Re-Energize Your Relationship

52 Brilliant Ideas
one good idea can change your life

Re-Energize Your Relationship

Reignite the Spark and Keep It Burning

Dr. Sabina Dosani and Peter Cross

A Perigee Book

A PERIGEE BOOK
Published by the Penguin Group
Penguin Group (USA) Inc.
375 Hudson Street, New York, New York 10014, USA
Penguin Group (Canada), 90 Eglinton Avenue East, Suite 700, Toronto, Ontario M4P 2Y3, Canada
(a division of Pearson Penguin Canada Inc.)
Penguin Books Ltd., 80 Strand, London WC2R 0RL, England
Penguin Group Ireland, 25 St. Stephen's Green, Dublin 2, Ireland (a division of Penguin Books Ltd.)
Penguin Group (Australia), 250 Camberwell Road, Camberwell, Victoria 3124, Australia
(a division of Pearson Australia Group Pty. Ltd.)
Penguin Books India Pvt. Ltd., 11 Community Centre, Panchsheel Park, New Delhi—110 017, India
Penguin Group (NZ), 67 Apollo Drive, Mairangi Bay, Auckland 1311, New Zealand
(a division of Pearson New Zealand Ltd.)
Penguin Books (South Africa) (Pty.) Ltd., 24 Sturdee Avenue, Rosebank, Johannesburg 2196,
South Africa

Penguin Books Ltd., Registered Offices: 80 Strand, London WC2R 0RL, England

While the authors have made every effort to provide accurate telephone numbers and Internet addresses at the time of publication, neither the publisher nor the authors assume any responsibility for errors, or for changes that occur after publication. Further, the publisher does not have any control over and does not assume any responsibility for author or third-party websites or their content.

First American edition: March 2007
Originally published in Great Britain in 2005 by The Infinite Ideas Company Limited.

Library of Congress Cataloging-in-Publication Data

Dosani, Sabina.
  [Re-energise your relationship]
  Re-energize your relationship : reignite the spark and keep it burning / Sabina Dosani and Peter Cross.—1st American ed.
    p. cm.
  Originally published: Re-energise your relationship. Oxford, U.K. : Infinite Ideas, 2005.
  "A Perigee book."
  Includes index.
  ISBN 978-0-399-53327-3 (alk. paper)
    1. Man-woman relationships.   I. Cross, Peter, 1952–   II. Title.

  HQ801.D747 2007
  646.7'8—dc22   2006047010

PRINTED IN THE UNITED STATES OF AMERICA

10 9 8 7 6 5 4 3 2 1

Most Perigee Books are available at special quantity discounts for bulk purchases for sales promotions, premiums, fundraising, or educational use. Special books, or book excerpts, can also be created to fit specific needs. For details, write: Special Markets, The Berkley Publishing Group, 375 Hudson Street, New York, New York 10014.

Brilliant ideas

Brilliant features

Each chapter of this book is designed to provide you with an inspirational idea that you can read quickly and put into practice right away.

Throughout you'll find four features that will help you to get right to the heart of the idea:

- *Try another idea* If this idea looks like a life-changer then there's no time to lose. *Try another idea* will point you straight to a related tip to expand and enhance the first.

- *Here's an idea for you* Give it a try—right here, right now—and get an idea of how well you're doing so far.

- *Defining ideas* Words of wisdom from masters and mistresses of the art, plus some interesting hangers-on.

- *How did it go?* If at first you do succeed try to hide your amazement. If, on the other hand, you don't this is where you'll find a Q and A that highlights common problems and how to get over them.

Introduction

"Give us the tools and we'll finish the job."
WINSTON CHURCHILL

In a relationship? Then this book's for you. You don't have to be married, straight, middle-aged, or old. You can be in an age gap relationship, come from different backgrounds and cultures, classes, clans, or castes, it doesn't matter. Nor do you have to wait until you and your relationship have become jaded and tired before trying these brilliant ideas. On the contrary, the earlier you sit down and think about your evolving life together the better.

We all spend so much time developing our careers, raising children, and creating gorgeous homes that we often neglect the most important person in our adult life and our relationship with him or her. There are so many books on the market promising that if you follow these or those rules you'll live in perfect harmony forever. If you're looking for a book like that, this isn't it. We make no promises about stopping arguments forever or never feeling angry with each other again. This is real life. We are here to promote possibilities, not pipe dreams. Forget rules; you need ideas. After all, just one good idea can change your relationship.

Here's the deal. We've got 52 Brilliant Ideas. You use them to invigorate your love life. So what other tools do you need to finish the job? We took a peek in our toolbox and this is what we found:

A pen and paper, for jotting down your own ideas, off-the-wall suggestions, and silly thoughts that might, just might, be worth trying. Even in this age of the laptop, an old-fashioned ballpoint still comes in handy for writing passionate love letters or making notes to plan for your perfect day out.

A ruler or tape measure, for measuring dissatisfaction, despair, and discord.

A protractor, to remind you that the best solutions to protracted relationship problems arise when you come at them from another angle.

A compass, because when you are truly lost this handy little object helps get you back in the right direction.

An eraser, to erase those bits best forgotten.

A set of scales, for weighing the pros and cons of each other's solutions and suggestions.

A hammer, to remind you that sometimes romance is elusive and there will be weeks when you just have to keep banging away.

A pair of pliers, so you don't forget that all relationships need regular tweaking and fine-tuning, and also to help you hang on to precious moments and memories that easily slip out of reach in the humdrum of daily life.

And finally, **a wrench,** to remind you not to throw it in the works.

You will find hundreds of things that you can do to improve your relationship. We have themed them together into 52 chapters. Some of these ideas will get you out of the house while others will keep you in. Some involve other people, others just the pair of you. As much as possible we have suggested possibilities that could be attempted by couples at any age of their lives and stage of relationship. We have road tested nearly all of them and had a lot of fun in the process. That doesn't mean we are experts in photography, ballroom dancing, cooking classes, and so on—just that we've given them a go.

Whether you use these ideas as suggested or adapt them to your particular circumstances doesn't matter too much. You might like to use them as a catalyst to develop your own thoughts and suggestions. If you are lucky enough to have an unlimited budget to re-energize your relationship, great. If, like us, you have more restricted funds, you'll be pleased to learn most of our ideas are inexpensive. We won't recommend any hot air balloon flights around the Valley of the Kings or weekend breaks to outer space. In relationships, thoughtfulness, time, and meaningful gestures matter more than money.

The most contented couples we know have a positive outlook and are players rather than spectators in the game of life. People, in other words, whose lives are full of diverse activities, types who work and play hard, who are excited rather than intimidated by change, and who look forward rather than back. This is a mind-set we've adopted and one we'll help you cultivate.

A bit about us: Between us, we've experienced passion, bitterness, excitement, jealousy, betrayal, exhilaration, divorce, boredom, and anger. Wherever you're at in your relationship, we've been there: Sabina's shouted, Peter's sulked. We've done our share of door slamming, bag packing, and swearing. Since then, we've found better ways, brilliant ways, of sorting out arguments, disagreements, and seemingly irreconcilable differences. And they work.

To outsiders, we sometimes seem an unusual pair. When we first met and fell in love, it was an inconvenient match, throwing together four cultures, an age gap of over two decades, and different values. Yet each of us recognized something in the other. We felt poured out of the same bottle, somehow made of the same stuff. And despite a few hurdles on the road to happily ever after, we've figured a few things out. Our different professional backgrounds, diverse friendships, and families have given us many great ideas to retain the sparkle. We know these 52 Brilliant Ideas worked for us, and they'll work for other people, too. People like you.

1

Read 'em and weep

Well-written love letters are powerful. But why does letter writing make us so inarticulate, mushy, and embarrassed? Why use stuffy Elizabethan when everyday English is a direct route to your lover's heart?

Yes, it's true: Writing love letters doesn't come as naturally as picking up the phone. Letter writing is an art form, but it's easier to learn than watercolor painting or French cooking.

Texting C U L8R is a pretty poor substitute for "I think that never in a thousand letters could I ever begin to tell you what it means to me to be able to come home to you. I never realized how starved I was for this wonderful sweetness," which is what Canadian writer Margaret Lawrence wrote to her lover Benedict Greene, just over fifty years ago.

Love letters are magical and are often treasured forever. But writing love letters is hard at first. By all means admire the lightness of touch of love letters penned by Alexander Pushkin: "Farewell; night is falling, and your image appears before me, all

Here's an idea for you . . .

You don't need to wait until you're away. Write a letter to the woman or man in your life and leave it for them when they come back from work or the store. Hide love notes in his suit pocket. Tuck them under her pillow or pop them in her pocketbook.

sad and voluptuous—I fancy I see your glance, your parted lips. I would give my life's blood for one minute of reality." But don't forget he didn't have any alternatives to snail mail.

There's nothing to stop you from enticing with equally erotic prose. "Fill your paper with the breathings of your heart," suggested the poet William Wordsworth to his wife. But how? Spend time thinking about your beloved, get comfortable, and start writing about what you were doing just before you picked your pen up, describe your surroundings and what's on your mind. Avoid cumbersome sentences when a simple word or phrase says the same. Start a new paragraph every time you change subject. It's that simple.

Maybe you're scared you'll sound crass or forceful. One myth about writing is that it comes effortlessly. Sometimes the muse will visit, but more often you'll have to coax her. Make a cup of tea, pour a glass of wine, put on some music, and start writing. Try including some of the following words: fascinating, touch, dazzling, enthralling, true love, longing, craving, yearning, sensational, kiss, soul mate, joy, heart, darling, stunning, lucky, enticement, and whole. If it's terrible, throw it in the trash and start again. Practice makes perfect, so don't be disheartened if you recycle a rainforest on your first attempt.

A common mistake is finishing letters with, "I've got to go now." Unless you want your partner to imagine you running to the bathroom, use a different expression. A short phrase that affectionately closes, like "all my love," "fondest love," "with love," "your lover," will work perfectly.

MORE THAN WORDS

Eighteenth-century love-letter writers used quill pens on special paper, sealed envelopes with wax, and tied letters with fine-looking ribbon. We can learn from them. Step inside a specialty stationery shop and you'll be stunned by the selection of writing paper. A letter written on crisp burgundy paper has more impact than the same words on the back of an envelope. Most people use blue or black ink; but why should you? Chocolate brown ink on thick cream paper helps your message sing. But be careful: green ink suggests poison and red ink might remind your loved one of corrected homework. Our friend Paul, a Navy medical officer, writes home on black paper using a silver gel pen. Jeanette, his wife, confided that she goes weak at the knees when these jewels flutter through her letter box. On her last birthday, he wrote in gold pen. Paul knows that letters are far more than a string of sentences. They're little gifts that Jeanette will keep for a lifetime, a part of himself that she can keep, reread, touch, and smell. Jeanette stores them in a special velvet box that would be the first thing she'd save in a fire.

Try another idea . . .

A picture's worth a thousand words. Why not illustrate your letters with pictures, drawings, or photos? See IDEA 41, *Snap, cackle, and print*, for practical hints.

Defining idea . . .

"Such a sweet gift, a piece of handwriting in an envelope that is not a bill, sitting in our friend's path when she trudges home from a long day spent among wahoos and savages, a day our words will help repair. They don't need to be immortal, just sincere. She can read them twice and again tomorrow: you're someone I care about, Corinne, and think of often and every time I do you make me smile."
GARRISON KEILLOR,
We Are Still Married

How did
it go?

Q It's all very well to suggest that I write love letters to my partner, but I feel smothered, nagged, and bullied by him. Can I tell him so?

A By all means write an angry letter, it's great therapy. Then set fire to it. Now you'll be ready to write something more loving.

Q I'm dyslexic and my handwriting is awful. Is there any hope?

A It's unfair, but poor spelling will distract your partner from your message. Type letters and use a spellchecker. If your writing is truly awful, cheat by using a handwriting font, or if you feel like splurging, pay a calligrapher. A professionally presented letter will probably be framed and cherished for years.

Q I've tried my best but I just can't write a decent love letter. I'd like to write like Homer's *Iliad*, but my stuff sounds more like Homer Simpson. Do you have any tips?

A Wrap a book of traditional love poems in handmade paper and copy one onto a matching note card. Spend time reading the poems out loud to your partner; it should help you develop a more classical style.

Search for the hero

We know the score. You fell in love with a hero and now your relationship isn't as wonderful as when you first met. We'll help you track down your partner's lost appeal.

Do you miss the good old days, when your lover listened spellbound to your stories, treated you like the sexiest creature on earth, and made you feel warm and fuzzy?

Have you heard that after the initial glow of romance, you're left with something deeper, more mature, that's, well, a bit boring really? That, once you've settled with your mate, spontaneity, romance, and heroics are just for birthdays and holidays? It's just not true.

Of course relationships change with time. As we get to know our partners better, we often love them more deeply and feel a closer bond. But this new companionship should be an add-on to the old intensity, not an instead-of. In the drudgery of our daily grind, it's often far easier to look for problems than solutions. At times it might feel as if the hero or heroine you fell in love with has sneaked off, leaving behind a dull replacement. We believe the hero is still there, waiting in the wings to be rediscovered and nurtured back to health.

Here's an idea for you . . .

Time for a little live experiment. Spend a day noticing and appreciating all your partner's mini heroics. Try to make at least twelve comments, like: "I love the way that even though you've been up half the night with the baby, you still look gorgeous." At the end of the day, spend a little time alone evaluating your partner's responses. We hope you're pleasantly surprised.

It takes a bit of effort to root out your partner's inner hero and you might have to look quite hard. We know that when you're in a rut of working, shopping, cooking, bringing up kids, cleaning, watching television, arguing, and worrying, it can be hard to believe there's a hero inside your tired, sniping partner. If that sounds familiar, we suggest you take half an hour for yourself, grab a sheet of paper, and answer the following questions:

■ Why do I love my partner?
■ What would I miss if we weren't together?

The tricky part is to then share your answers with your partner. Instead of attaching your list to the fridge, sneak your responses into conversations. For example, if you love your partner's sense of humor, instead of just laughing at her jokes, try making a comment like, "I like it when you make me laugh. Nobody makes me laugh like you do." Or, if you appreciate hubby getting your kids to stick to bedtime, say something like, "I love the way you're a really hands-on dad. I couldn't have gotten the kids to bed without your help."

PEEL OFF THE LABEL

Everyone, your partner included, lives up or down to others' expectations. Try to avoid labeling your partner. If you think "he's not romantic" or "she's always late," you're less likely to notice the times when he does buy roses or when she arrives ahead of you.

If your girlfriend usually leaves you to do the laundry but one day does the ironing on a whim, resist the temptation to make a sarcastic comment like "Are we expecting the president for dinner?" and instead try "I really like it when you iron the shirts" (and don't tell her she's missed a bit).

Nobody can be a knight in shining armor every day, so as well as noticing the big stuff, show appreciation for small acts of kindness. Say your partner has put off hanging a picture you were both given months ago. You come home one day and notice it up. Most of us would instinctively say something along the lines of "I'm glad that picture is finally up." The problem with that sort of comment is that it stresses the negative and sends your partner the message that he's a bit of a procrastinator. Hardly heroic. But if you breeze in and exclaim, "Oh that looks fantastic. I really like the way you've hung that," he'll feel like a hero inside and be more likely to act like one. It's crucial to watch your tone as well as your turn of phrase, so that you sound more like an impressed temptress than a disappointed schoolmistress.

Try another idea . . .

When your partner comes home, give him a hero's welcome—give him a massage. We'll show you how in IDEA 24, *Reach out and touch.*

Defining idea . . .

"I remember a lovely New Yorker *cartoon, so poignant I cried. The drawing was of an obviously poor, overweight, and exhausted couple sitting at their kitchen table. The husband, in his T-shirt, had not shaved. The wife had curlers in her hair. Dirty dishes and [diapers] hung on a makeshift clothesline strung from a pipe to the fridge. They were drinking coffee out of chipped old mugs. The caption was the man smiling at his wife, saying, 'I just love the way you wrinkle your nose when you laugh.' "*
LEIL LOWNDES, relationship expert and author

7

Q **My wife has really let herself go over the years, lounging around in old leggings and being lazy around the house. I'd love her to be the way she was when we first met, but making positive comments feels like an act. How can I be natural and honest with my wife, without feeling phony?**

A *Sorry to be so frank, but you are going to have to act differently to get her to change. The suggestions we've given have worked for others in your predicament, but you need to find your own words and voice. It's so much easier to stick with what we know. If you're used to making comments that start with "I wish you would . . ." and "Why don't you ever . . . ," then this new approach will feel alien for a while. But, like learning to ride a bike, it'll get easier with practice and will become second nature to you.*

Q **I try so hard to notice and point out all the nice things that Clive does, but he just doesn't reciprocate. What can I do?**

A *Negativity is infectious, but so is a positive attitude. Someone has to make the first move, but if you're resentful or begrudging he'll pick it up. Stick with it and once Clive feels more like a hero, he'll behave like one.*

3

A walk on the wild side

Walking is wonderful. Need to clear your heads of clutter and put problems into proper perspective? Take a hike. Chances are you'll walk out with a problem and come home with a solution.

Whether you saunter in companionable silence or amble in animated conversation, nothing quite matches a daily constitutional. It's an escape from domesticity and a chance to reconnect with the person who matters.

LET'S BE PEDESTRIAN

Unless you live in an offshore lighthouse, there is always somewhere to walk. The sort of journey we're talking about does not need to have a specific purpose or destination, though it might involve the collection of a newspaper or be broken up by a drink at a local bar; the real reason is to have a change of environment and a change of air. Open spaces have mind-expanding properties that help you to think more clearly; all of a sudden, difficulties become more doable and problems less problematic. Walking boosts your level of serotonin, the feel-good chemical in our

9

Here's an idea for you . . .

Next time you find yourself getting into an argument, why not suggest you go for a walk together to take time out and regain your composure? You might agree not to discuss the contested subject, or do so only after an interval of, say, half an hour.

brains. It also releases the body's natural opiates—endorphins—giving you a buzz. When we walk with our partners we associate feeling high with him or her.

As we know all too well, small spaces can be constricting and close down creative processes. We love our walks. We take one most days, and sometimes even more frequently if we are working from home. You could say we are blessed, what with being a short distance from a river and a wonderful park. But even when we are not at home, we still walk: in the countryside, by the sea, in every village and town there is always something to see, hear, touch, and feel. Life is different on foot, the pace is slower, there are fewer distractions, and you don't have to worry about parking, drunk driving, or one-way streets.

MARCHING ORDERS

If one of you feels like walking, go for a walk together. Walks give couples a chance to talk and think. And on warm summer evenings a chance to stop and drink. And it goes without saying that a walk will make any meal eaten afterward all the more enjoyable.

Defining idea . . .

"I have two doctors—my left leg and my right."
ANONYMOUS

MEMORY LANE

Walking can perk up your relationship in different ways. Perhaps, like many couples, you went for more walks in your "courting days." Going for walks, years or even decades into a relationship, may take you not only down Pineview Avenue, but down memory lane as well. Indeed, if you make the same journey, retracing forgotten steps, those old passionate feelings will probably return.

Walking is a great date, and it's free. For more on free love, check out IDEA 43, *Cheap thrills.*

Try another idea . . .

TWO'S COMPANY, THREE OR MORE IS A RAMBLING ASSOCIATION

Many couples find that joining a walking club gives them a sharper focus and opportunities to meet like-minded saunterers or strollers. If there isn't a club within a short walking distance from your home, why not start one?

"Where'er you walk, cool gales shall fan the glade. Trees where you tread, the blushing flow'rs shall rise. And all things flourish where you turn your eyes."
ALEXANDER POPE

Defining idea . . .

But if asked for a definitive reason for walks and why we continue to do so, one word comes to mind: serendipity—the faculty of making happy and unexpected accidental discoveries. Sometimes it is what we discover in the environment: a new building site to spy on, an unexpectedly lovely garden, a misspelled ad in a shop window. More often, the happy discovery is something one of us says, triggered by something we have seen. A walk is a journey into your partner's head and heart.

"I like long walks, especially when they are taken by people who annoy me."
FRED A. ALLEN, radio comic

Defining idea . . .

11

How did it go?

Q **You've almost convinced us, but nobody walks around here. If our neighbors saw us walking somewhere they'd wonder what was going on and tongues would start wagging. What do you suggest?**

A *Our first thought is forget the neighbors! Seriously, though, would it matter? If you are really worried about it, why not drive somewhere, park, and walk from there? Once you've been for a few walks, what others think won't seem so important. You could, of course, get a dog.*

Q **I'd love to go for walks with my husband. The trouble is, he's very unfit and gets out of breath walking the short distance down our driveway to the car. How can we go walking yet avoid the constant threat of widowhood?**

A *We suggest you start by parking the car a bit farther down the road each day, to gradually build up his fitness. Then move on to driving somewhere pretty and going for short and then longer walks. Give it three months and you'll both be able to stride with pride as you leave the car behind. Stick with it, as improving your husband's fitness will have myriad benefits for your love life.*

4

Where's the party?

Never invited to decent parties? Time to mix your own magic ingredients and play the happening host. Plus you'll get to air your finery and drink your guests' fine wines.

Memorable parties are not about fancy food, expensive wines, and identical napkin rings. Great gatherings are about people, passion, and unexpected pleasure. Recharge your relationship as you refill guests' glasses.

So how does hosting a party help your relationship? For starters, you have to sit down and agree on all the fine details. Who will you invite? Will the Browns get along with the Patels and the Joneses? What will you cook? What will your budget be? Will you be buying brandy or just cheap bottles of red and white? There may be conflict, but this is useful in getting to know your partner better. If you're the partner usually burdened with shopping, cooking, and cleaning after parties, it's time to make a list of chores that could be shared. Learning to ask your partner for help is an important love lesson, and a social night in that is important to both of you is a prime time to try it out. Team up and work together during the preparation,

Here's an
idea for
you . . .

You don't need an occasion for a celebration. Go on, invite over a happy couple you admire. Find out their secret for long-term loving over a few beers and lasagne and linger over their food for thought.

cohost the proceedings, and you'll come away with bucket-loads of happy reflections.

Hosting parties is enormously satisfying. They give both of you opportunities to be loving, supportive, kind, and creative. Jointly hosted parties held at home tell the world something about you as a twosome. Whether you're fun and quirky, elegant artists, or suave sophisticates, few things equal the pride and pleasure in giving other people a really enjoyable meal and experience, or introducing couples or singles you hope will like each other and seeing those relationships blossom. Playing party host or hostess is also an extremely good way of finding new interests away from the workplace or golf course.

DINNER PARTIES

Whether it's a cozy dinner for four or a sophisticated sit-down for sixteen, we've discovered that top-notch food isn't the most important ingredient in a dinner party recipe for success. Fabulous food helps, but good company, a relaxed inclusive environment, and interesting conversation are far more important. Some couples worry that their home and dining facilities don't measure up. Remember those fun parties eating from a plate balanced on your knees in tiny dorm rooms? Bet you didn't complain about drinking wine from plastic glasses then. That said, if you're helping her wow important clients or schmooze with special business associates, it's easy to create a meal that screams, "we're a stylish duo." Eat by candlelight, scatter some red rose petals over a

Defining
idea . . .

"You know I hate parties. My idea of hell is a very large party in a cold room, where everyone has to play hockey properly."
STELLA GIBBONS,
Cold Comfort Farm

16

crisp, white tablecloth, and show off the family silver. Sparkling wine practically guarantees sparkling conversations. Entertaining your partner's colleagues means you'll at least know who he's talking about when he grumbles about Ed or Kevin's less fine points. Most people spend half their waking lives at work, so we think it makes sense to share our work lives with our other halves.

Don't leave your guestlist to guesswork. Check out IDEA 35, *With a little help from your friends*.

Set a mellow mood with background music. IDEA 15, *Music, the food of love*, will help hit the right notes.

Try another idea . . .

. . . and another

LAZY LUNCHES

For a lazy but lush laid-back lunch, forget soup and sandwiches, and think sushi, dressed crabs, little vegetable tarts, blueberries, and thick slabs of dark chocolate. Chocolate is the ultimate love drug, raising levels of a brain chemical called serotonin, which is responsible for making us feel happy. Team these naughty nibbles with easy drinking wine or fruit smoothies. Relax, add a good pal or two, and let the good times roll.

SAY CHEESE

Slaving over a soufflé in a hot kitchen is no fun. Up the glam factor by ditching dessert and serving a ripe, runny brie and some firm, juicy grapes.

"Two's company but three's a couple."
ADAM PHILLIPS, psychotherapist

Defining idea . . .

17

How did it go?

Q **We'd love to entertain but our tiny apartment is so small that there's only just enough oxygen for the two of us. Any suggestions?**

A *You could rent the back room of a restaurant or a small hall. Then again, you could link up with friends with larger places and offer to buy and cook food using their equipment, with a mixture of guests both you and they select.*

Q **My husband has just been promoted. There's a tradition that the head of the department, which he now is, throws an end-of-summer get-together for the rest of the team. I don't want all his colleagues poring over our possessions or smoking in the house, but I don't want to display big No Smoking and No Looking signs either. How can I keep them in line while keeping a smile on my face?**

A *Why not have a barbecue and put up a tent in the backyard in case it rains? This sort of informal gathering has a lot going for it. Wandering around with a plate of food seems to make everyone more relaxed and informal as they are able to pass the time away with colleagues they want to be with and avoid the ones they don't.*

5

It's in his kiss

If you believe a kiss is just a kiss, you've been conned. It's such an intimate act that prostitutes never let clients kiss them (allegedly). Want to recapture the closeness? Pucker up.

Every teenager knows kisses are an end in themselves, not just a preliminary to sex. There's mileage in them there lips.

LUCKY LIPS

We tend to be conscientious when it comes to countering smelly breath, reaching for mints or sprigs of parsley if we've eaten onions or garlic, but how many of us pay as much attention to the state of our lips? Call us sexist, but women tend to be better at looking after their lips than men (which may be why they're called chaps). So guys, if you're tempted to skip this section, stay awhile. Chapped, rough, or scratchy lips are a major turn-off. Instead, think silky, supple lips, ready to take you wherever you want to go. Women get it wrong, too, by overcompensating with lots of lipstick. It may be a good look for performers, but not for performance kissing. A daily slick of balm or flavored gloss should keep your lips in perfect kissing condition. But avoid applying it just before going into action—slippery lips make for sloppy kisses. If your lips are very chapped, try exfoliating them gently by covering

Here's an idea for you . . .

Set aside at least fifteen minutes and have a no-tongues kissing session that doesn't lead anywhere else. Rub your lips together, kiss the corners of her mouth to make your partner smile, and enjoy all the new and forgotten sensations.

. . . and another

Kissing and embracing is a vital part of any re-energizing campaign. Start today and make kissing part of your daily routine. Practice kissing hello and good-bye, and take it from there.

them in balm and rubbing softly with a toothbrush. Now, down to business. In books, kisses are often described as greedy or hungry, as if one person is eating the other. By all means nibble, but never swallow.

When you kiss, think about how you move your lips. Let them dance a little, playing with different degrees of friction and tension. Nibble, squeeze, or trap your partner's bottom lip or tongue. Mess around and have fun.

FRENCH KISSING

We know you've had a few tongue tussles and we're not out to teach you any basics. But if you don't mind, we'd like to pull you over for a speed check. Slow and romantic or fast and passionate, the speed of a kiss tells you a lot about the kisser's intentions. As a general rule, we suggest warming up and starting slow. Changing speed mid-kiss should be like changing gear, smoothly and at appropriate times. Try not to clunk or over-rev. Of course, sometimes we all like the thrill of going from zero to sixty in three seconds, but not when we've just woken up.

Defining idea . . .

"They look at each other with their mouths. They look at each other with their whole bodies."
MURIEL RUKEYSER, poet

MILLIONAIRE'S KISSES

Add glamour, style, and fizz to a humble kiss. Take a sip of champagne, hold it in your mouth, and kiss your partner. Chilled bubbles on your lips and tongue introduce an extra dimension. For a less bling-bling version, try a frozen cocktail with a fizzy mixer.

KISSING IN THE BACK ROW

One reason kissing is so popular with teenagers and older illicit lovers is the danger involved, the heady excitement that comes with the fear of being caught. Committed couples often get to a stage when this pleasure is lost and physical intimacy is taken for granted. Why not re-create early tension by having furtive kissing sessions in semi-public places, like elevators and movie theaters?

KISS AND TELL

Kissing's not just for lips. Rediscover your partner's body. You know about the importance of kissing places like the insides of elbows, between the shoulder blades, and the backs of knees; to discover your partner's secret kiss-spots, you'll just have to ask and hope they kiss and tell.

If all that kissing gets you into the groove, try adding some background music. See IDEA 15, *Music, the food of love.*

Try another idea . . .

"Animals can be tamed, but not mouths."
DONALD WINNICOTT, pediatrician and psychoanalyst

Defining idea . . .

"If I profane with my unworthiest hand. This holy shrine, the gentle fine is this, My lips, two blushing pilgrims ready stand, To smooth that rough touch with a tender kiss."
WILLIAM SHAKESPEARE

Defining idea . . .

21

How did it go?

Q **Kissing takes my breath away. Literally. I've got recurrent sinusitis and can't breathe through my nose. I'd like to try some long kisses, but I just can't hold my breath long enough, and if I try too hard I end up snorting like an elephant seal. What can I do?**

A *Looking a bit breathless can be sexy, but being chronically short of breath isn't. Work some air breaks into your kissing. Try short intervals where you kiss her neck, hair, or ears before moving back onto her lips.*

Q **I'd like to have more passionate kisses but I'm worried that my breath smells. How do I kiss with confidence?**

A *As you probably know, smelly breath is usually caused by bacteria growing in mouths. To find out if your breath really does smell, lick the back of your hand and sniff. That should give you a pretty accurate idea of what your partner's treated to when you kiss. If regular brushing and flossing don't help, it's time to visit your dentist. Mints may help in the meantime.*

6

Petal hard

If you need something to push the buds of your relationship into bloom, we've got just the thing. Want your love life to blossom? Say it with flowers.

Whatever your sentiment—striking, sensual, sanguine, or sexy—there's a stem out there that will say it for you. Smell is our most powerful sense, arousing all sorts of memories and primal urges.

You can't go wrong with roses. Velvety crimson petals exuding the heady smell of rose. Reeks of seduction, doesn't it? Orchids, jasmine, and lilies are also renowned for aphrodisiac scents. But wilted daffodils, suffocating in their cellophane wrap, are best left at the gas station. Flowers ought to be bought from markets, or plucked from your own garden.

Lots of people make the mistake of thinking flowers are just for women. Sending pots of purple pansies to the building site where your lover is foreman might not go over too well, but take it from us, get it right and you'll always be his favorite flower. A shallow bowl of succulents will be well received and looks macho in most

Here's an idea for you . . .

If you've left it too late and all you can find is a wilted bunch at the twenty-four-hour store, shame on you. But, hey, all is not lost: Take everything out of the wrapper and remove any ties. Pick out all the droopers and toss them. Cut off any brown or decayed parts from the remaining flowers. Better already, isn't it? Now put them in a bucket of fizzy mineral water, or still water with soluble aspirin. Empty your fridge and shove the bucket in for about half an hour. If you've time, see if you can do a hand-tied bouquet; otherwise, just rewrap. By the time you hand it to your beloved, it should look stunning. No guarantees for the morning after, though.

workplaces. Their round, sensual shapes survive weekends without water.

Why don't you fill some empty glass jars with cut flowers? You can use coffee jars, pasta sauce containers, or jam jars. Soak off the label, fill it with water, and put in some blooms. If you cram the flowers in tight, it doesn't matter what you use. They don't have to be store-bought. Even daisies and buttercups look fantastic. Either distribute the jars randomly around your home or group them in threes in the dining room, on the mantelpiece, or on the bedside table.

While you're at it, is there any way you can personalize your floral gift? Jan is a chemist. Previous boyfriends had been put off by her long hours in the lab. Her boyfriend Clive grew a pot of gerberas on his windowsill and then put twelve single stems into water-filled test tubes in a test-tube rack. She was pleasantly surprised, but also understood the subtext: "I understand your job is important and I support you." Jonathon gave his partner a terra-cotta pot of sprouting sunflower seeds. On the pot he wrote, "My love for you keeps growing." Corny, but it worked. Elsie's husband of forty-three years was feeling miserable and unattractive after chemotherapy. He was delighted with her present: a Venus flytrap with a little note, "You're still a great catch."

To be really successful with flowers, you need to be au fait with the hand-tied bouquet. It is a bit tricky at first, but you don't need sixteen weeks of advanced floristry classes to get the hang of it. Just follow these six steps. It's worth the effort:

- Put the stems in a bowl of water and, using a sharp kitchen knife, remove all the side-shoots and leaves that will be underwater when the bouquet is in its vase.
- Choose one striking flower and hold it upright in your left hand (or right hand, if you are left-handed).
- Add a few flowers. Make sure that the flower head is to the left and the stem is to the right. As you add flowers, twist the flowers a quarter of a turn.
- Continue adding flowers a few at a time and twisting. Twisting makes a spiral stem so the flowers stand upright.
- When you have run out of flowers, tie with ribbon at the place where you were holding them in your left (or right) hand.
- Wrap more ribbon round the stem if you want to. You can use raffia, wire, or twine instead of ribbon.

Has all that flower arranging made you hungry? Find out how to prepare the ultimate food of love in IDEA 39, *You are what you eat.*

Try another idea . . .

"People from a planet without flowers would think we must be mad with joy the whole time to have the things about us."
IRIS MURDOCH

Defining idea . . .

"When a man brings his wife flowers for no reason—there's a reason."
MOLLY MCGEE, comedy radio show character

Defining idea . . .

How did it go?

Q **My girlfriend is allergic to flowers. Should I buy her some silk ones to stop her from sneezing and wheezing?**

A *Forget artificial flowers—would you like to eat plastic chocolate?—but you're right to think of silk. We suggest you start memorizing her measurements and buy her lingerie instead.*

Q **The thing that stops me from buying cut flowers, other than the cost, is that they will die and look dreadful within a week. Can you suggest alternatives?**

A *Have you thought of getting a dramatic potted plant instead? We suggest a calla (or arum) lily. You could have it both ways: Cut off a single stem and present it to stun her on that day, and give her the plant for her to remember you by every time she looks at it.*

7

My favorite things

Birthdays, anniversaries, and holidays. They seem to come around more quickly every year. But what do you give the partner who's got everything?

If all of your previous presents have passed their pleasure-by date, be inspired by our contemporary take on traditional tokens of affection.

GIFT BASKETS

We can't think of a present that better captures what celebrations are all about. Pamper your partner with a gift basket that reflects her individual style, tastes, and interests.

For example, if he's a football fan, cover a box with pictures from a football magazine and fill it with a ticket to see his team, a football jersey, chocolate-covered footballs, or memorabilia, like a season ticket from the year he was born. Wrap it in his team colors. If she's a cyclist, prepare a package of bike accessories: a map of bicycle routes, cycling shorts, a personalized water bottle, or a new bicycle lock. Is your lover a shopaholic? If you don't know her sizes, slip a gift certificate for her favorite shop into the handbag she's been drooling over all season. Wrap in a silk scarf and fasten with a brooch.

Here's an idea for you . . . **Instead of one big present, try five small ones—one for each of the senses: smell, taste, vision, hearing, and touch. And the perfect card? Store-bought or homemade? You'll have to use your sixth sense for that: intuition.**

THEME

How about giving presents according to traditional wedding anniversary themes? You don't have to be married. Use them to celebrate the anniversary of when you first met, first moved in together, or first smiled at each other across a crowded train. Or your partner's third birthday since you've been together. You don't need a book like this to tell you that traditionally the twenty-fifth anniversary is silver, fortieth ruby, and fiftieth gold, but what about the earlier ones? Here are some brilliant gift ideas, but don't forget that every year is special.

First: paper

Surprise him with personalized notepaper. Think thick and creamy, embossed with his monogram or family crest. No family crest? Design one of your own. Alternatively, you could have your bedroom redecorated in new wallpaper. This could be a bit risky or seriously risqué, depending on how well you know your lover's interior design tastes. Books, book tokens, or any paper gift certificate also make good gifts.

Second: cotton

Imagine this: You've had a bad day at work, someone made a snide comment on the subway, you came home, and were whisked into a bed that had crisp, fresh, Egyptian cotton bedsheets, monogrammed with your and your partner's initials. Just because he remembered it was two years to the day since you met. Why not have a shirt made to his measurements? Some tailors will add a small label with a personalized message.

Third: leather

You can go any way you want with this one: a pair of fitted leather jeans, a flattering pencil skirt, or thigh-high boots. And for the guys? Wallets are always welcome, especially if you slip something inside. If your partner is sentimental, a photo of you or a little note is sweet. But be warned, the more materialistic may be left wanting.

Fourth: linen

Choices, choices: Will you update bed linen, choose a gorgeous tablecloth and serve a memorable meal on it, or pledge to do all her laundry for a year?

Fifth: wood

Our friend Simon surprised his partner by making a wooden love seat for the backyard. If your carpentry skills aren't up to it, cheat and buy one. If you're looking for something smaller, how about a carved box in which to store love letters?

Sixth: iron

A wrought-iron bed or a trouser press. What would your partner rather have? You know him better than we do.

Seventh: copper

Shiny pots or pans? Don't tie him to the kitchen sink. Plant a copper beech tree in the garden. In a high-rise apartment? A bonsai tree with copper-colored leaves will do the trick.

Still stuck for that perfect present? Take your partner shopping. Abroad. See IDEA 32, *April in Paris*. All you need now is your credit card.

Try another idea . . .

29

Try another idea . . .

Give your gifts in style. Find out more in IDEA 37, *What a difference a day makes.*

Eighth: bronze

Treat her to a fake tanning treatment, or better still, a holiday where she'll develop a real one.

Ninth: china

A bone china dinner set for twelve, or if you're too boho for all that matching stuff, hand paint a dinner set at a ceramics shop. Alternatively, you could take him on a trip to the Great Wall of China.

Tenth: aluminum

Send your partner to the skies with a flying lesson.

Eleventh: steel

Time for some edgy, urban jewelry or artisan cutlery. Or develop nerves of steel with matching piercings.

Fourteenth: ivory

How about piano lessons, or even a baby grand? Busts your budget? Ours, too, but dream a little and go to hear a live pianist in concert instead.

Defining idea . . .

"A wedding anniversary is the celebration of love, trust, partnership, tolerance, and tenacity. The order varies for any given year."
PAUL SWEENEY

Thirtieth: pearl

Only a certain sort of woman wears twinsets and pearls. We're not saying there's anything wrong with that, but if it's not your partner's style, or if you're treating your fella, how about taking in a performance of Bizet's *Pearlfisher* opera? Or, if the budget can stretch that far, a vacation in Bahrain?

Q **We're coming up to our twenty-fifth wedding anniversary and the family is getting together to buy us something special. They've asked us what we want, but we don't have a clue. Do you?**

How did it go?

A *Travel broadens the mind and revitalizes long-term relationships. Once you've been together this long, experiences are more important than material things. Why not ask for tickets and see the world on the Orient Express or a cruise ship?*

Q **I'm not sure whether to buy an anniversary present just for my partner or to get us something for the home. Any thoughts?**

A *We'd go with both. Buy yourselves something you'll both enjoy but exchange small personal gifts, too.*

8

French kissing in the USA

Long-distance relationships can be legendary. Too often, they're lackluster. Whether you're working on opposite sides of the country or living on different continents, we'll save your relationship from long-distance doldrums.

Even the strongest relationships can crumble if one of you is away working, serving with the armed forces, or in prison. How can you keep your love alive until your next joyful reunion?

SHE'S LEAVING HOME

Unless, like our friend Bernice, you met your soul mate at an airport just hours before both jetting off in different directions, you'll probably have some time together before doing any long-distance loving. Sorry, but you do have to talk about your impending separation. It's tempting to avoid it, but most problems happen when there are misunderstandings. If you secretly expect your partner to "surprise" you with spontaneous visits or to pick you up from the airport, unless he's telepathic you're gonna feel let down. You also need to work out how you'll communicate across time zones and other barriers. Peter works away at a prison for part of the week, where security prohibits mobile phones. We negotiate a time he'll call so

Here's an
idea for
you . . .

Make a tangible reminder of your relationship for your partner—a tape or CD of "your" songs, a personalized photo album, or a framed photo of the two of you.

Sabina doesn't wait by the phone. If your partner's not behind bars, a videophone may be a viable and attractive option—especially if you've got an attractive partner. How about a weekly e-mailed photo diary? Maybe it's time to get blogging? Or invest in a home DVD recorder, to send clips and comments in the mail. On a more practical note, it can save a lot of hassle if you work out a household budget, especially if the main earner is working away. Staying in touch over a distance is expensive and needs to be factored in. Worries strain relationships, so the less hassle, the happier you'll be together. In long-term relationships, people tend to get a bit dependent. If this sounds familiar, swap skills. If you both know where your fuse box is, how to clean out a drain, or check the car oil level, you're less likely to panic when you're home alone. And we know it sounds morbid, but we suggest making wills. All that travel cranks up your chances of a premature trip to the undertaker.

WISH YOU WERE HERE

After saying good-bye, don't put your own life on hold until your partner's back. Bob felt like missing the Rodin exhibition because Connor wasn't there to share it, but went anyway, had a ball, bought an exhibition catalog to share when Connor returned, and sent a postcard of his favorite sculpture, *The Kiss*.

Defining
idea . . .

"I wish that you were here or that I were there, or that we were together anywhere!"
ANONYMOUS

Parcels and packages are terrific treats and a wonderful way to share things with your partner while she's away. How about mailing a book you've just enjoyed or a disposable camera with a little note: "I'd love to see the view from your window"? When Marie went to work in Zurich for a year, she sent her partner regular small souvenirs, including a weekly bar of Lindt chocolate. It made their separation sweeter. Boris's wife uses as her screensaver a photo that he e-mailed her—some beautiful tulips from Amsterdam.

Out of sight, out of mind? Turn to IDEA 18, *Bewitched, bothered, and bewildered,* so you don't succumb to temptation.

Try another idea . . .

I JUST CALLED TO SAY I LOVE YOU

Soaring phone bills? Do it the old-fashioned way. We'll help you write a perfect love letter in IDEA 1, *Read 'em and weep.*

. . . and another

If you're slavishly predictable, your partner might feel short-changed, but with a bit of invention, you'll be irresistible. Why not vary your communication methods and style: a playful e-mail today, an erotic text message tomorrow, perfumed love letter on the weekend, quirky quips on an unusual postcard midweek. As well as planned communication, be spontaneous. If you've agreed to call every Friday, call on Sunday night one week, too, just to say "I love you."

HELP, I NEED SOMEBODY

"We are the perfect couple, we're just not in the perfect situation."
JOEY RIVETT

Defining idea . . .

Never call in a crisis. We know it's counterintuitive, but consider this: The roof's falling down, there are rats in the basement, and you've locked yourself out. You're right to reach for the phone, but call the locksmith, roofer, and rat-catcher rather than your lover. It might make you feel better, but there's not much he can do in Sydney if you're suffering in San Francisco. He'll just fret, which could strain your relationship. Instead, call him when you've sorted it out, and rather than ranting about your problems, rave about your solutions. Sassy independence is sexier than needy misery. Whatever your gender, be a fixer and mender.

REUNITED

How much time it takes to readjust to being together can come as a shock. You're used to making decisions alone and suddenly need to compromise and do things jointly again. So if your life feels invaded by a relative stranger, don't panic. Find some time to chill out and share stories and experiences.

How did it go?

Q **We live in Connecticut. My partner works in New York during the week. I get used to my own company and space. I so look forward to him coming home each Friday, but get irritated with him talking all about his week at work and we end up arguing. Any suggestions?**

A *Sounds like you need to plan your hellos as much as your good-byes. Why not develop a Friday-night welcome-back ritual that lets you both ease into a different routine? A relaxing stroll around your neighborhood, champagne in the bath, and snuggling up in the back row at the movies are just a few of the sort of low-key ways you can get used to each other's company again.*

Q **My partner is a musician. I find it difficult when she goes on tour. I'm angry when she leaves but miss her terribly when she's not there. What should I do?**

A *Why not indulge yourself a little when she's away? Have a night in with the friends that she least gets along with. Be self-sufficient and develop some interests she doesn't share. That way you'll both have adventures to compare when she comes home.*

9

Vacation romance

Whether it's backpacking in the foothills of the Himalayas or being pampered at an all-inclusive exclusive Thai spa, you can use a vacation to inject a little romance into a jet-lagged love affair.

Of course vacation romances aren't just for teenagers. Yet all too often, rather than being a lover's retreat, vacations stress our relationships. Perhaps it's time to do it differently.

REASON FOR THE SEASON

Whatever the weather, there's a perfect trip to recharge your love batteries. Spring is a time for renewal and growth; a perfect time for a reviving tour. Whether you opt for the informality of a family-run B&B or the intimacy of a stylish rented apartment, discover a new city together to learn new things about each other.

So the sun's shining and the sangria's flowing? Make the most of soaring temperatures and heat up your relationship. Miles of sandy beaches are perfect for holding hands and strolling. Or laze by the pool in skimpy clothes, give him your best sultry look, and coyly ask him to rub suntan lotion into those hard-to-reach places. You won't be out of reach for long.

Here's an idea for you . . . **Make your partner's eyes twinkle. We know a couple who always tells the hotel it's their anniversary. Many upgrade them to a room with a better view or bigger terrace, and even if they don't leave a complimentary magnum of champagne, they'll usually provide drinks on arrival, a bowl of fruit, flowers, or a special cake.**

Or how about an autumnal adventure? Horse riding, biking, or climbing will all leave you drenched in adrenaline, a key re-energizing chemical. Or spend a week on a craft course in the country, perhaps learning about upholstery together. If your relationship's felt a bit frosty, don't suffer a winter of discontent—warm up in a winter wonderland. There's nothing like cozying up in a comfy chalet before getting down to some après-ski in the hot tub.

DREAM DESTINATION OR DICEY LUCK?

"Where do you want to go this year?"
"I don't mind, where do you want to go?"
"I don't know. Why don't you choose?"

Sound familiar? Vacation couple trouble often has roots in different expectations. It pays to establish what each of you wants. Are you yearning for a peaceful escape or a daring adventure? A short trip or longer, more leisurely leave? Struggling to work out what you want? Think about your last vacation together. What worked well and what would you like to do differently this time? Compare your fantasy vacations and try to combine the best of both. If you're stuck, it's time to get the dice out. Write down your three top destinations each and number them one to six. Flip a coin to decide who gets to roll the dice, and . . . you've guessed it . . . the dice decides your final destination.

We suggest you agree on a holiday budget. Agreeing on an upper limit for your trip, any presents, going out, and souvenirs may seem excessively anal, but the bottom line is that it helps you leave money problems at home while you're away. The more you both think it through, the better you'll enjoy your destination. Tackle questions like: Where will our budget come from? Are we willing to go into debt, and if so, by how much? Whose credit card will we use?

Want to get away but can't get time off work? Enjoy a weekend detour. Find out more in IDEA 32, *April in Paris*.

Try another idea . . .

BOOK A VACATION

Plan a vacation that revolves around your partner's favorite book. Track down restaurants, nightclubs, cafes, and other places mentioned. How do they measure up in real life? Kieran loves *A Room with a View*, so Helen arranged for them to travel around Italy. Lidia and Poonam went to Moscow for their anniversary after both enjoying *Death and the Penguin*. Dick wrote his dissertation on Dickens's *Tale of Two Cities*. His girlfriend Elise helped him celebrate his Masters by taking him to London and Paris. They had the best of times . . .

"If you wish to travel far and fast, travel light. Take off all your envies, jealousies, unforgiveness, selfishness, and fears."
GLENN CLARK, founder of Camps Farthest Out

Defining idea . . .

How did
it go?

Q **My partner Janette works in Dubai. We hadn't seen each other for seven months and were both really looking forward to being together when I flew out for a ten-day vacation. Why did it bomb?**

A *Spending time together on unfamiliar turf when you haven't had much of a chance to reconnect can be a recipe for disaster. Next time you plan a visit, we suggest you use some of your letters, e-mails, and phone calls to explore each other's expectations before you go.*

Q **Every year my husband Andrew and I get stressed out over our Christmas break. We receive invitations from both my mom and my dad, who have both remarried. My husband and I are also expected to eat a full Christmas dinner with his birth parents and with his adoptive parents. We rush around eating four Christmas dinners in two days, feeling frantic, fat, and frustrated. Inevitably we take it out on each other. How can we have a happy holiday without feeling pulled in different directions?**

A *This year, come up with an action plan with Andrew well before the invites start rolling in. You might decide to visit in a four-year rolling cycle, invite them all to your place, or go into hiding until the mistletoe's come down. Presenting your own plan to well-meaning family is far more productive than reacting to theirs. It's hard, but you won't be able to keep everybody happy. If you keep compromising, resentments will grow and strain your relationship. Concentrate on your partner and do whatever supports your relationship best.*

10

Money, money, money

Money matters. Your attitude toward dollars in your purse, change in your pocket, or credit on your plastic can mean boom or bust for your relationship.

The love of money may be the root of all evil, but opposing values about money can have the same impact on couples as diesel in a regular gas engine.

As your accountant likes to tell you, without regular review, the best financial plans have a tendency to go sour. To keep your love life in credit, we suggest working through the key questions every six months. Go on, write it in your planner.

If opposites attract, chances are that one of you is a bit of a miser, the other, a big spender. You don't have to be an heiress or a compulsive gambler to have heated arguments over money. Money talks, and talking about money is vital for a thriving relationship. Although some of us would rather visit the dentist or have an all-over body wax, you need to have honest discussions about how to handle your incomings and outgoings. What will you spend, save, share, invest, insure, and retire on?

Here's an idea for you . . .

Sit down with your partner and think through the following questions. You might like to commit your responses to paper: How much capital do we need? Are we happy with our household economy? Are we spending beyond our earnings and savings? What changes can we make? What is our monthly budget and how can we help each other stick to it? How can we plan for retirement?

Dual-income couples may be best off with his, hers, and ours accounts for personal and household expenses. If you do decide to have an "ours" account, how will you both contribute? Going Dutch may seem the fairest option, but a pro-rata scheme may be more equitable if you are a billionaire and your partner's not. If you're both earning, beware of putting all your money in one account. Your Botox bill may be better kept a secret. A shared debit card also makes it harder to buy surprise presents for your partner.

PUT YOUR MONEY WHERE YOUR SPOUSE IS

When Peter decided to freelance full-time, we had to readjust our expectations about what we could splurge with or set aside. Chances are that at some stage during your relationship, one of you will work part-time, be laid off, set up your own business, or take time out from the rat race. What changes are you ready to make to your standard of living?

Defining idea . . .

"We talk about the quality of product and service. What about the quality of our relationships and the quality of our communications and the quality of our promises to each other?"
MAX DE PREE

CALLED TO ACCOUNT

However you decide to manage money in your relationship, we suggest you keep household accounts. That way, if you fall into the red, you'll see where the money's hemorrhaging and be able to stem the flow quickly, rather than arguing over whose fault it is.

RELEASING CAPITAL

There might be money in them there closets and kitchen cupboards. Admit it, they are full of clutter you know you'll never use again. But one man's trash is another man's collectible item. The record was replaced by the CD years ago, so why hang on to that Led Zeppelin LP? Who knows, it might be worth a few bucks on eBay. Too painful? Put the money you raise into a special "treats" account and have an occasional blow-out in a favorite restaurant.

WHERE THERE'S A WILL, THERE'S A WAY

Many couples think wills can wait. If you're living together or have children from previous relationships, it can be doubly nightmarish for your partner if you die intestate. Play fair with each other and make your wills together. At the very least, it's a great way to review the other important people in your lives. And you might even enjoy deciding who should next inherit the stuffed tabby Great-Aunt Agatha left for you last year.

Down to your last dollar, yen, or euro? Relationships can be revamped on a shoestring. Take him on a cheap date. See IDEA 43, *Cheap thrills.*

Try another idea . . .

"*Money can be at the root of lots of small-print clauses. Who earns it, how it is spent and saved, and what it means to each partner. You may have reason for saving every penny at twenty-five but is it still applicable at forty-five? Spending priorities can also be a source of confusion. This is especially true if one of you tends to want to save and the other to spend. Unspoken contracts can sometimes force one or another into agreeing to spend or save for years ahead.*"
From *How to Stay Together Forever* by JULIA COLE, writer and therapist

Defining idea . . .

How did it go?

Q **My partner is incredibly stingy. He earns three times as much as me, but I always have to pay for nice stuff for our home. We go halves for necessities, but I even have to buy my own flowers. Why is he so mean?**

A *Maybe he's worried about being in debt. It sounds as if you have different risk tolerances. Ask him and talk it through.*

Q **I love my wife Victoria, but the way she spends money makes me go ballistic. She's a full-time mom and I'm the only earner. The other day I came home to find builders extending the kitchen. Why should I foot the bill for these major outgoings without discussion?**

A *The short answer is, you shouldn't. Victoria is treating your salary and savings as disposable income—but you are letting it happen. Overspending is her problem, not yours, but unless you act, you're condoning her overspending. Send the builders packing and refuse to pay up any more unless you've both agreed. It will be hard and at first there may be major arguments. We know a couple in very similar circumstances, and when one partner refused to pay up, their phone was temporarily cut off and there were red faces as shops turned down credit cards.*

11
Truly scentsational

For lasting love you need more than common scents. We'll show you how to reach the sweet smell of relationship success by following your nose.

Educationalist Jean Jacques Rousseau called smell the "sense of imagination." It is the sense most closely related to memory, and learning a little about its science will help you score well in your relationship.

YOUR OLFACTORY FACTORY

Did you know you have forty million olfactory receptors (tiny nerve endings that pick up chemical come-ons) up your nose that transmit impulses to your hippocampus? The hippocampus is the bit of the limbic system of your brain that deals with memory, learning, and emotion. That's why particular aromas retain special meaning and can evoke powerful memories even after decades.

*Here's an
idea for
you . . .*

Delicious food smells are welcoming and nurturing. But if, like us, you don't have time to bake every day, cheat by burning sticks of vanilla incense in the kitchen.

*. . . and
another*

It's easy to have a harmonious relationship when the sky is blue, the sun is shining, and you're basking on a golden beach. Ever thought that feeling ought to be bottled? Well, hey, it has. Give each other a massage with last year's suntan lotion and transport yourselves back to Hawaii.

OF MOTHS AND MEN

Just over fifty years ago, a group of German scientists was looking at some silkworm moths. They found that a certain chemical, which they called a pheromone, made the moths very frisky. Twenty years later, and after studying 500,000 female moths, they hit the jackpot. They'd isolated a compound that made male moths beat their wings in a sexual dance. So what? you might well ask. Well, like moths, we also produce chemicals that arouse our partners. Men's and women's pheromones smell different. Men's sweat is more acidic than women's, so male pheromones have a more musky quality than female ones. Musk, an ingredient commonly used in perfumes, is a top turn-on for women. So now you know what to look out for on those aftershave and cologne bottle labels. And smelling lavender, doughnuts, licorice, oriental spice, and cola can all increase blood flow to the penis. If you don't want to put eau de doughnut in your oil burner, you might be interested to read that essential oils cinnamon, jasmine, musk, patchouli, rose, sandalwood, and vanilla are the sexiest members of the aromatherapy dynasty. They're believed to stimulate the release of neurochemicals, triggering sexual responses.

*Defining
idea . . .*

"The best smell in the world is that man that you love."
JENNIFER ANISTON

King George III banned perfume, allegedly after "women of ill repute" used it to seduce men. Luckily for us, he's dead now, so there's no excuse for not making the most of it. There are hundreds of different bottles and price tags out there, but more or less all fragrances fall into one of the following categories:

Learn how to give a massage that will leave your partner quivering in IDEA 24, *Reach out and touch*.

Try another idea . . .

- Green: like a walk in the lush countryside on a crisp, clear day
- Oceanic: like the sea
- Floral: girly, pretty, and pleasurable
- Oriental: spicy, heady smells that take you on exotic journeys
- Woody: to remind you of that night in the forest
- Fruity: like, um, fruit

"You could never have a relationship with someone whose smell you didn't like."
MARGARET MEAD, anthropologist

Defining idea . . .

Did your mom tell you to apply perfume to your wrists? Good, but other pulse points, like your navel, collarbone, behind your knees, or on your ankles, often get overlooked. Do you know the worst place to apply scent? Behind your ears! There are no sebaceous glands there, so the alcohol will wrinkle your skin. For peachy rather than pruney skin, match your body lotion and perfume. In fact, layering, as the beauty pros call it, is the best way of making scent last. Use perfumed shower gel or bath essence, then body lotion or powder, before spritzing with eau de parfum (that's the concentrated one) and freshening up during the day with eau de toilette.

CANDLE IN THE WIND

Create a super scent-sual environment by lighting scented candles all around your home. Soft light and suggestive smells will get you both into a peaceful, loving mood. As a general rule, men like pine, sandalwood, and frankincense, while women often prefer rose, lemongrass, or ylang ylang. But we believe rules were made to be broken, so play around and find out what chills you both out or turns you on.

How did it go?

Q   I'd like to buy perfume for my girlfriend, but how do I choose?

A   *Any perfume has three components. Top notes are released when it first touches her skin; the body reveals itself when perfume mixes with your girlfriend's body chemistry; and the bottom note is the final expression of the fragrance as the scent becomes hers. As you've probably realized, the way a certain perfume smells to you at a counter may be totally different from the way it smells on her. While it might seem romantic to surprise her with a beautiful glass bottle, you're best off taking her with you when you go perfume shopping. A few tips: Get your girlfriend to try out smells on her skin, not on those little cardboard strips. If she sniffs straight after spraying it on, she'll mostly smell alcohol. This might remind her of you, but it's best to wait awhile to see what the body and bottom note smell like. And it sounds obvious, but trying too many out in one day can get a tad confusing. Three seems optimal.*

Q   I'd like to smell good (in a masculine way) for my partner, but don't know where to start. What do you suggest?

A   *Why not experiment with scented shampoos? They're cheaper than colognes, and hair that smells good is a real turn-on. Zesty smells like orange, grapefruit, and lime are refreshing, whereas musk, sandalwood, and oak moss are more obviously erotic.*

12

Undercover agents

Lace or latex? Satin or silk? Your underwear is an effective relationship barometer. Excuse us while we rummage through your laundry, but sorting out your unmentionables can make a big difference.

Is your underwear slinky and seductive, casual and comfy, or frayed and faded? Instead of rethreading the elastic into those graying boxer shorts, switch to sexy underwear and develop a sexy attitude.

A BRIEF LOOK

People didn't wear knickers until the nineteenth century. The word is adapted from knickerbockers, those men's trousers that fasten at the knees. We know your knickers don't come down to your knees, but do they do any more than just keep out the cold?

Why not go through each other's underwear drawers and give some of the residents a new lease on life as dusters? Of course, it's hard to tell what they look like when they're lying in the drawer, so draw the curtains and get modeling.

FOR YOUR EYES ONLY

At the start of relationships women tend to wear matching bras and briefs, lace body suits, and slinky camisoles. And men make sure their underwear is clean. A few years down the line, we make the mistake of thinking we can get away with any old graying, fraying, baggy granny panties, because they're out of sight. No matter how long you've been together, knowing your partner is wearing underwear she looks fantastic in can give you both a little thrill. We're not saying flash your undies, but try giving him a little glimpse of your bra that has a captivating little detail like an embroidered dragonfly or sequins. Or let your partner know that under that somber gray business suit, there's a shot of her favorite color.

THIGH HOPES

Panty hose are ugly. Nothing puts a damper on a relationship faster than a glimpse of flesh-colored nylon wrinkling at the crotch. So whether you want to wear fishnets, lace tops, or sheer, keep him in suspense with suspenders and hold up your relationship with held-up hosiery—start stocking shocking stockings.

Defining idea . . .

"You know it's a bad day when you put your bra on backwards and it fits better."
ANONYMOUS

MEASURE UP

Most women are wearing the wrong size bra, which can be uncomfortable and unattractive. You could go and be fitted professionally in a lingerie shop, but it's much more fun to do it together at home. Here's how: Get your partner

50

to measure around your rib cage, directly under your bust. Adding five inches gives you your size. If it's an odd number, round it up to the next even one. Now the fun bit. Ask him to measure around the fullest part of your

Dressed like a diva? Now create a boudoir fit for lingerie loungers. Check out IDEA 33, Bedroom eyes.

Try another idea . . .

bust. And the sums: compare the two numbers. Every inch difference is a letter size. So if you're 28 inches around your rib cage (plus 5 makes 33, rounded up to 34) and 34 around your bust, you're a 34A. If you're 31 inches around your rib cage (plus 5 makes 36) and 40 inches round your bust, you're a 36D.

SHOPPING TRIPS

When you're buying lingerie or underwear for your partner, the trick is to choose something that they'll feel good in, rather than give you the hots. If he feels uncomfortable in the all-in-one Tarzan suit, it won't give your relationship the wild edge you hoped for. If your wife is romantic at heart, selecting something pink and pretty is a better bet than crotchless leather fetishwear.

"There's a fine line between where the sexy underwear stops and the back pages of top shelves magazine begin. Cross it and enjoy yourself."
MARION MCGILVERY, author of *Aphrodisiac*

Defining idea . . .

GOOD FOUNDATIONS

Underwear represents the secret and intimate side of your relationship. But the right

"Brevity is the soul of lingerie."
DOROTHY PARKER

Defining idea . . .

underwear can affect the way you look and feel in your outerwear, too. When you choose underwear for yourself or your partner, think about what they'll wear it under to avoid an ugly visible panty line.

How did it go?

Q **My girlfriend wears an old T-shirt in bed. I've bought her some sexy nightgowns, but she says her T-shirt is more comfortable and won't wear them. How can I persuade her to try them?**

A *Perhaps they weren't her style. But we agree that an old T-shirt isn't going to up the romance factor. If she's after comfort, why not buy her a soft, brushed cotton nightshirt or a pair of silk pajamas?*

Q **I'd like to buy my wife some underwear but I don't know where to start. I've thought of asking a store clerk, but I don't want to look like a dirty old man in the women's lingerie section. What can I do?**

A *Why not buy online? Next time your wife is out, have a peek in her underwear drawer to find out what she already has. If you buy something too far out of her range, she'll barely wear it. As well as looking at labels to get exact sizes, pay attention to her bras. Does she like underwire or padding? Cotton or other materials? Look at the cut of her panties. Does she wear low rise, briefs, or thongs? Once you're armed with styles and sizes, browse a number of sites. Many of them show underwear on models, so if you're choosing a color, see how it looks on a model who has similar hair and skin color to your wife. If you can get it gift wrapped, too, all the better.*

13

Stormy weather

If only relationships—and life—were all smooth sailing. They aren't, and couldn't be. Too much change, too much stress, too much turbulence. Here's our chart to navigate you through the choppy waters.

Some relationship books claim that arguments can be banished from your life. Just read the sacred text and by applying the guru's simple rules, you and your partner will never fight again...

An outrageous claim, and were one of us to make it, the other would get very angry and turn red. Arguments happen in the best households, but they don't have to end in tears, tantrums, or broken china.

STAY UP AND FIGHT

Arguments are part of life and love. At best, they can spur you on to change aspects of your relationship or make you notice that your partner is unhappy. At worst, serious sulking or screaming sessions can drag on for days, becoming aggressive power

Here's an idea for you . . .

The trick is to preempt problems before they escalate. Next time you find yourself getting angry and about to indulge in a little plate throwing, call a break to calm down. Let your tempers cool, then try to deconstruct what has been going on in a more relaxed atmosphere. There's a way of doing this where everyone's a winner. It takes about half an hour, a bit of patience, and goodwill. Each of you have five minutes to put your point of view across. Your partner has to shut up and listen for those five minutes. Then it's his turn. Next, work together to come up with a choice of possible solutions. Discuss the pros and cons of each until you reach one you can both live with. You will both have to be prepared to compromise.

struggles, and leaving you hurt and ground down. Disagreements can actually give your relationship a boost rather than lead to a breakup if you follow these rules for a good fight:

- Prevention is better than cure. If you always end up arguing about household bills, draw up a budget you both agree with.

- Discover what you're actually arguing about. Most arguments happen because of disagreements about work, money, sex, or children. If you can resolve how you both feel about these topics, you'll live in blissful harmony. Unfortunately, it takes most of us a lifetime.

- Forget about point scoring.

- Use words, not fists. If it gets violent, get help or get out.

- Insults, put-downs, critical comments, sarcasm, and humiliation are all below the belt.

Defining idea . . .

"Never go to bed in a bad mood. Stay up and fight."
PHYLLIS DILLER, comedienne and writer

- Compromise. If seeing your partner's socks on the floor makes you seethe, make a deal. Bargains like "I'll wash up if you take the trash out" are less likely to cause fallouts than "You lazy pig. Clean up your own mess or go back to your mother."

- When you've both calmed down, sort out the reason behind your argument. For example, if you've argued about the phone bill, find a time to talk about it.

- Say you're sorry when you hurt your partner.

- Forgive your partner for hurting you and forgive yourself for being unkind.

- Make up before you go to sleep.

Bickering and snapping at each other lately? Make up in style: Head off for a romantic weekend. See IDEA 32, April in Paris.

Try another idea...

"At this present moment I have a strong urge to go over there, wrap both his legs around his neck, and stick his suede shoes in his mouth. But I suppose that would only be termed a temporary solution."
From *Sisterly Feelings* by ALAN AYCKBOURN

Defining idea...

"Relationships carry the whole universe within them. They can be everything, nothing, here, then gone. One moment, loving someone makes you shine; the next it feels like matter and antimatter colliding."
From *Guide to Intuitive Healing* by JUDITH ORLOFF

Defining idea...

How did
it go?

Q **Simon and I find ourselves fighting over stupid things. Last week an epic battle was triggered by where I squeezed the toothpaste tube. We both know our reactions are out of proportion and can see them coming, but to no avail. What can we do to stop hurting ourselves?**

A *There is no right or wrong way to squeeze toothpaste, hang toilet paper, or open a boiled egg. Most of us, however, opt for one preferred way and expect our partner to do the same. Why not just try to acknowledge the differences? It's okay to tell your partner of their foibles that piss you off as long as you make it clear it is your problem rather than theirs.*

Q **Jean and I have been together for four years. We don't make love nearly as often as we used to. Now we seem only to have passionate sex after an argument. Surely it can't be right?**

A *Sounds like your sex life is a bit flat and mundane and an argument adds fuel and ignition to the dying embers. Maybe you need to find other ways to crank up your passion. Try a scary film as an alternative method of foreplay.*

Q **We argue a lot and I do most of the shouting. I feel better afterward and it clears the air. My partner wants me to lower my voice but I can't express my anger like that. Isn't it better out than in?**

A *Shouting at your partner might make you feel better but it's not much fun for him. He probably feels blamed and confronted during your arguments, which is bad news for your relationship. So bite your tongue and get rid of your pent-up feelings by knocking a tennis ball around or hitting a punching bag.*

14

Should I stay or should I go?

Love life hit an iceberg? How do you know when to hang in there and salvage a wrecked relationship and when to swim for new shores?

Call us die-hard romantics, but we believe most relationships are salvageable. Even after betrayal, arguments, debt, or months of sexual drought, it's possible to recapture the spark and ignite something rich and purposeful.

Even the best relationships feel like sinking ships sometimes, and the urge to escape with the nearest lifeboat can be strong. But the decision about whether to stay in a lackluster love affair or find a new port in the storm should be a rational one.

Resist making decisions on a whim. Even if you've caught your new bride in bed with your best man, stay put. Sometimes you'll find yourself changing your mind from day to day, or even hour to hour. In truth, many people who leave relationships impulsively later regret it, only to find it's too late to return. You've probably invested many months or years in your alliance. Parents, in-laws, and friends will all give you their views, but it's not really any of their business. They've

Here's an idea for you . . .

When it's hard to decide whether to stay or go, it's usually because both options have a lot going for them. Whatever you decide, an informed choice is better than an impulsive one. When you have a moment, make a list of what first attracted you to your partner. What are her good qualities? What would you miss? In what ways does she bring out the best in you?

all got their own agenda, so we suggest you avoid discussing your dilemma until you've reached your decision.

WRITE STUFF

Writing your thoughts down brings clarity and helps you decide. Try keeping a diary of thoughts and feelings. What do you want from your relationship? Why do you feel like leaving? Is it your relationship that is making you unhappy or could there be other reasons, like a career crisis or mounting debts? If there has been a catastrophe, like infidelity, be honest with yourself about what your relationship was like before. Do you have something worth saving or were you thinking about leaving anyway? If your relationship was good before, you may well decide to give it another go. See if you can discover what your partner wants. Even if your problems seem insurmountable, good intentions on both sides go a long way. Can you see the difficulties as a catalyst for change?

What can you do if you are incompatible? Charlie wants six children, but Denise doesn't want any. Russell wants a pet tarantula and Sally's arachnophobic. Stephanie wants to live in a city, but Jo's a committed country dweller. George wants sex twice a day, Jenny would be happy with twice a year. As we said, we're die-hard romantics and we think we can reconcile most so-called irreconcilable differences with goodwill, compromise, and imagination. But romance alone won't do. It takes both of you to look at problems and come up with creative solutions. Charlie retrained as a child-care provider. Sally had her phobia treated and has grown rather fond of Gideon the tarantula. Stephanie and Jo live in a country-style cottage in a small commuter town. And Jenny and George? Don't be so nosy—that's their business!

Can't see anything good about your partner? Check out IDEA 2, Search for the hero.

Try another idea . . .

Having said that, we've identified four relationship scenarios that are bad news. There's no point staying together if:

HIS PANTS ARE ON FIRE

Persistent liars cause big trouble. Relationships are about trust. Can't believe a word he says? Get packing.

HE'S MAD, BAD, AND DANGEROUS TO KNOW

Rachel's partner Damien was convinced she was having an affair. She wasn't. He hired a private detective to follow her and then accused her of bribing the detective to lie on her behalf. He went through her laundry, checking her underwear for semen stains. Every day when she came home he interrogated her about where she'd been. This sort of jealousy is rare and is a sign of illness, often related to hitting the bottle. In the trade it's called Othello Syndrome. Rachel was advised to get out of the relationship, as there was a risk that Damien might kill her. If this sort of behavior sounds at all familiar, get out and get expert help for your partner. You may be able to re-energize your relationship, but your partner needs treatment first.

"There is nothing permanent except change."
HERACLITUS

SHE SUBJECTS YOU TO DEGRADING TREATMENT

If she persistently puts you down in public or humiliates you in front of your friends, don't stand for it. Nobody deserves to have his or her self-worth eroded by an insecure person who helps themselves to feel better by making their lovers look stupid, useless, or inept.

HE'S HITTING HOME

You can't salvage your relationship if your partner is threatening, hitting, or sexually assaulting you. Domestic violence happens in every sort of relationship, and is hardly ever a onetime thing. Sometimes it's there from the start; sometimes it won't surface for years. Lots of people stay because they are frightened, or hope things will improve. But it usually gets worse over time. Get out and get help from the police, a doctor, or a local helpline.

Q **My partner and I have grown apart over the years and have little in common. We've both had affairs and been gratuitously cruel to each other. We've stayed together for the sake of our three children, who are now all teenagers. But have we made the right decision?**

How did it go?

A *This is a tricky one. The jury is still out on whether it's better for children to live in a war-torn household or for their parents to separate amicably. Nobody wins in an acrimonious split, but if you can separate and stay friends, it might be a better option. Alternatively, you have nothing to lose by trying to find some common ground.*

Q **My father-in-law died a couple of years ago and I agreed that my mother-in-law could move in with us. Since then our relationship has gone from bad to worse. We never have any time to ourselves and my wife always takes her mom's side during one of our frequent fights. I'm at my wit's end. I've started going to a bar most evenings and use any opportunity to stay away from home. What should I do?**

A *This sounds serious. Clearly you need to talk to your wife, preferably away from the home environment, and let her know how you feel. Giving her an "either she goes or I go" ultimatum might put her in an impossible position, but perhaps together you could find a creative solution, like re-housing your mother-in-law nearby, before matters get even worse.*

15

Music, the food of love

For the definitive turn-on, turn on some music. Shakespeare called it the food of love. Whether Handel or hip-hop–edged neo-soul is your thing, play on.

Mozart, Motown, or Madonna: so much magnificent music to push your partner's buttons. Isn't it time you put aside the familiar and experimented with something new?

For centuries, music has helped lovers find each other irresistible. It doesn't have to be Bizet's *Carmen*. Even a catchy little tune can help you explain, entertain, and explore. A jam session at your local bar, a little bit of soul on a wet Sunday afternoon, or some R&B can rekindle feelings from your debut days and help your relationship make a comeback.

(PASSION) KILLER TUNES

Let's face it, anyone who expects a karaoke evening to liven up their love life is likely to be disappointed, but there are other, less obvious, turn-offs. What's your music of choice? Like us, you and your partner may have diverse tastes. Perhaps you like Purcell and Puccini while she's mad for Peter Gabriel? Or he plays Albinoni on a

Here's an idea for you . . .

Next time you go watch a film that moves you and brings you closer, buy your partner the soundtrack. Listening to it will bring back strong feelings and help you hold on to the intimacy.

loop, while you long for some Abba or Atomic Kitten? One thing's for sure: Just as overexposure to a particular piece or artist breeds discontent, overexposure to your partner's CDs or tapes is grounds for a divorce. If Jimi Hendrix turns you on, but not your partner, try turning it off sometimes.

MUSIC IN THE BEDROOM

A quarter of a century ago Dudley Moore starred as a hapless composer infatuated by Bo Derek in the film *10*. For many, the highpoint in this farce was the use of Ravel's *Bolero*, a slow, rhythmic orchestral piece that builds and builds to a huge crescendo. Accepting that Ravel and Moore both reach their climax about fifteen minutes later than most men, there is a serious point here: music in the bedroom can enhance your and your lover's experience. In the mood for love? Set a slow and smoochy mood with gentle lyrical piano music, like Erik Satie, Chopin, or Schubert. Heat up the action with some fire and passion from Wagner, Motorhead, or James Brown. Develop your love muscle with disco sounds or dance tracks. You'll also need some blissful stuff to gently bring you down when you are in that heavenly post-coital stupor afterward. The libidinous blend in Miles Davis's "Kind of Blue" makes many lovers feel kind of wonderful. If you don't care for all that jazz, Mozart's arias never fail to take you to another plane.

FIREWORKS MUSIC

Music ignites passions. You probably remember that when you were first together, the ideas and feelings you had for your partner were echoed in song lyrics played on the radio. So many songs seemed to have been written just for the two of you. Those feelings aren't lost, they are just smoldering embers. It's easy to rekindle some sparks. Potent and poignant memories stick to songs we associate

All those tunes got you tapping your feet? Ready to move together when the music moves you? See IDEA 26, _Let's face the music and dance._

Try another idea...

with the early heady days of romance. Jenny only has to hear a few bars of the "Birdie Song" before remembering why she fell in love with Xavier, re-experiencing his allure and feeling weak at the knees all over again. If you've been feeling disconnected and have missed the excitement of the early days, we suggest you play a song that reminds you both of your budding romance. It might be the first tune you smooched to, an aria from *Cosi fan Tutte,* or the classical track from a carpet cleaner commercial he liked to hum along to when you first lived together. We don't guarantee fireworks, but it will certainly fan the flame.

JUST THE TICKET

Next time your partner casually lets slip that she loves that tune, do a bit of homework. Find out who it's by. Surprising your partner with a pair of tickets to hear her favorite crooner belt out some ballads is a first-rate way to crank up the volume in a fading relationship. Even if dreary loverman balladry doesn't bring tears to your eyes, buying her the album to remember the concert by is a fine ploy. And if hippyish world music makes his world go around, slum it at an outdoor festival, pitch a tent, and get your relationship back in tune.

"Music I heard with you was more than music,
and bread I broke with you was more than bread.
Now that I am without you all is desolate;
all that was once so beautiful is dead."
CONRAD AIKEN

Defining idea...

How did it go? **Q** **I think buying my partner music is a great idea. Unfortunately I am to musical taste what Mother Teresa is to female beauty. I'm tone deaf and don't know where to start. Do you have any suggestions?**

A *It's easy to tune in to your partner's preferences with a bit of subtle detective work. Establish what radio stations he listens to and get to know their playlists. Once you know whether it's rock, reggae, or Rachmaninov he's into, recruit the help of a music store assistant, who'll be only too eager to show off her intimate knowledge of the genre.*

Q **How can I wean my man off Black Sabbath and Meatloaf? It's driving me crazy—I feel like banging my head against the wall repeatedly.**

A *You can't. Chances are he hates some of your music, too. Why not talk to him about your musical incompatibility and suggesting he has a heavy metal night in while you go out to listen to something lighter?*

16

Venn I fall in love

Stuck in a rut? Every discussion ending in an argument? When you're feeling flustered, fed up, foolish, and frustrated, it's time to return to the drawing board.

Ever felt stranded in your own bubble? Isolated from your partner and drifting ever farther away? Don't go around in circles. Draw some overlapping ones instead.

You know that feeling. You're marching along happily and all seems well. Then almost imperceptibly two minds, that often feel like one, fall out of sync. Bickering replaces quiet contentment, irritation sets in where before there was pleasure in your partner's utterances. Grab a pad and pen and a couple of hours away from distractions.

STEP ONE

Both partners should draw two large overlapping circles. One circle represents each of you and the overlap represents things or qualities that are common to you both. This exercise can be used or adapted to any areas of your joint life. You can use it to focus on your finances, social life, thoughts on children, pets, attitudes to parents and in-laws, careers, or vacations. In each of these areas, the stuff in the overlap of your Venn

Here's an idea for you . . .

If you find that you find yourselves arguing about the same topic? Why not make it the focus of a Venn diagram exercise? Fighting over lack of funds? You should each list your own preferences for where the money should go and see what can be moved into a central overlap section.

diagram is the glue that sticks you together. These might be shared values, interests, or relationships with friends, but they're the things that make you both happy. At a glance, you'll see your partner's opinions and your own, as well as how they think things are, from your perspective. If there are sticking points, rather than being overwhelmed by a topic like money, a Venn diagram breaks it into smaller chunks that you can address more easily.

Tom

golf, crime fiction, and watching boxing

TV, especially *Friends* and the news, watching football, cycling, darts, bars and drinking, and going to comedy clubs

clothes shopping, reading chick lit, TV soaps, and talking to Sheila on the phone

Jerry

STEP TWO

Spend about fifteen to twenty minutes filling in these Venn diagrams as comprehensively as possible. Tom loves golf but Jerry hates it, so Tom's put golf on the outer edge of his circle as far from the center as possible. They both enjoy darts and so write darts in the overlap. You can also include names of friends you have and haven't in common, places, TV programs, books, films, newspapers, even politics. The more wide-ranging and specific you can be, the better.

STEP THREE

Share and compare. You might be surprised at how different or similar your partner's diagram is from your own. Time for some home truths. Some things will self-evident while other items need to be qualified. "I put your mom in my section because I like her and get along with her and you don't." Comments like this give you insights into the way your partner thinks and feels.

STEP FOUR

Now it's time to look at the overlap and brainstorm ways of focusing on what you've got in common. If you both hate washing dishes, is it time to buy a dishwasher?

STEP FIVE

Again using words in the overlap, try to deconstruct mutual interests. What is it about darts you both find so attractive? Is it being competitive, being a member of a team, the banter in the bar, or representing the bar in competitions? This sort of questioning generates ideas for other shared interests. If it's the competitive part, what other games could you play and enjoy together? If it's the involvement with your local community, how else can you get involved?

For alternative ways of thinking about your partner and your relationship, why not look at IDEA 2, *Search for the hero*?

Try another idea...

Your Venn diagrams indicate that you both would like to be more sociable, so turn to IDEA 4, *Where's the party?*

...and another

"Similar values keep the love coals warm long after the first flames of passion have cooled."
LEIL LOWNDES, relationship expert and author of *How to Make Anyone Fall in Love with You*

Defining idea...

How did it go?

Q I think putting ideas on paper is a great way of moving forward but my partner thinks it is the sort of stupid suggestion you'd find in a women's magazine and he refuses to play along.

A *Some people hate the idea of writing anything down. Maybe they rarely write and feel self-conscious about poor spelling or bad handwriting. In this instance you might consider adapting the exercise and having a discussion covering the same ground in a particular shared interest with a view to generating ideas for other things that you could do together.*

Q This is more a thank-you than a question. My partner and I used your idea and did a Venn diagram about our friends. Maybe I'm losing it, but I had no idea that Brian disliked some of the people I thought were joint friends. We also came to realize that we both like Simon a lot more than we thought and have had him over to dinner since and are really pleased that we have gotten closer to him. This exercise worked for us. Thanks.

A *Thank you.*

Jealous guy

Banishing jealous feelings is bound to revitalize your relationship. Recognize them and act.

Jealousy's a funny emotion. The object of your desire wanting you all to him or herself can be strangely seductive, for a little while. But once the glorification has worn off, relentless jealousy grates.

Here's why. Your partner's jealousy has nothing to do with you. She's suspicious not because you're such a gorgeous hunk, but because she feels like a useless frump who can't possibly hang on to anyone. So if you've felt flattered by your boyfriend's jealousy, forget it. It's about his controlling power, not your pulling power.

Jealous partners make us feel like caged lovebirds: trapped and aching to fly away at the earliest opportunity. Maybe you've been censoring conversations, seeing friends less, or are afraid of provoking a watchful partner into one of her rages. Jealous lovers are usually deeply insecure. But take heart. Once you understand that their possessiveness isn't a sign of your desirability but comes from a need to be loved

Remember, jealousy is about power and control. If your partner is jealous, chances are she controls most aspects of your life together. It's time to redress the balance. For example, if your wife usually decides where you go on your family vacation, be assertive and explain that you would like to choose this year. Maybe your boyfriend has chosen the last six cars you both own. Go to some car dealers together and show him what you are buying next.

and to control, you can tame the feral green-eyed monster.

Soon after Jack and Tina got together, she went to visit her mother in France. "Jack phoned me three times a day," recalls Tina. "At first I was touched and thought he missed me. After a couple of days I realized he was checking up on me and was jealous of the good time I was having." When Tina came home, she confronted Jack, who admitted he was afraid she would run off with a Gallic god. After she reassured him she wasn't looking elsewhere, they struck a deal. No phone calls during the day, except if there was a life-or-death emergency. Jack learned to trust Tina and his jealous feelings were checked before getting out of control.

If your partner's jealous, try Tina's trick. Pick a time when you are getting along well and stress how his jealous behavior makes you feel, rather than blaming your partner. Comments like, "It's not my fault your ex-wife ran off with your granddad," are only going to spark an argument. Instead, ask your partner if he's worried you'll find someone else. Reassure him only once and then explain what you need him to do differently so you don't feel stifled or stalked.

Joshua was jealous of his boyfriend Fred openly checking out other guys. He alternated between telling him off and sulking, sometimes for days on end. Then he tried something different. Joshua started pointing out guys that he thought Fred would like, saying things like, "Hey Fred, check out that six-pack." When he shared Fred's not so sneaky glances, he felt included and wasn't jealous.

Sometimes, despite any evidence, people cling to the belief that their partner is having an affair. This is rare, but can get dangerous. Sound familiar? See IDEA 14, *Should I stay or should I go?*

Try another idea . . .

Let's be honest. Window-shopping, eye candy, whatever you want to call it—everyone looks at other people sometimes. Most of us are just discreet enough not to get caught. If you and your partner can agree on a "look but don't touch" rule, there isn't any need to feel threatened. If you can go one step further and point out other people your partner will probably like, what relationship expert Leil Lowndes calls giving "guilt-free snacks," the green-eyed monster will turn into a green-eyed house pet. In Leil's words, "If he has his guilt-free gander, you will have a much happier goose."

"It is as absurd to say that a man can't love one woman all the time as it is to say that a violinist needs several violins to play the same music."
HONORÉ DE BALZAC

Defining idea . . .

How did it go?

Q **My husband's possessiveness has gotten worse over the years. He controls our finances, so I can't choose our vacation destinations or family car. He books restaurants from work and tells me what to wear when we go out. I don't want to leave him because, other than his control issues, he's got a lot of good qualities. I know I need to take back some control, but nothing seems to work. What should I do?**

A *He is probably a kind but insecure guy. It sounds as if you need to start small. Try to win some control back every day. For example, if he insists on choosing the restaurant, make a point of picking up the wine list and ordering drinks. Agree to go to the movies, but book tickets in advance for your chosen film. And get dressed at the last minute, when it's too late to change if he doesn't approve. You should also cultivate some interests of your own. It will be difficult at first, but once he survives your decision making, you should notice him being less envious and, who knows, he may well find your independence exciting.*

Q **My husband of twenty-five years left me for a much younger woman. I'm in a new relationship now, but keep worrying that my boyfriend will do the same thing. I can't bring myself to trust him, but he's getting really fed up by having to account for every moment he's away from me. I don't like feeling jealous all the time. What can I do?**

A *It's hard not to feel jealous when trust has been broken, but give this new guy a break. If he didn't like you better than every other woman, he wouldn't be with you. Try this: Every time you want to ask him for reassurance or feel jealous about where he has been, try to remind yourself that he's chosen to be with you and nobody else, that he hasn't left you and hasn't shown any signs of wanting to. Remind yourself he isn't your ex. It might take a couple of months, but once you get the hang of it, you'll be less clingy, which is always more attractive.*

18

Bewitched, bothered, and bewildered

Flirting with the milkman? Exchanging glances with your guitar teacher? Daydreaming about running away with your wife's best friend?

Having a crush on someone else is not, in itself, a bad thing. A frisson of safe excitement can brighten office life, and casual flirting makes a mundane journey or chore a lot more enjoyable.

The danger, if there is one, is located at home. Almost imperceptibly the passion and sparkle that once existed in your domestic life can leak away like water from a punctured swimming pool and re-emerge elsewhere. You might have seen it yourself: people who are the life and soul of the party or public bar becoming bores or bullies behind their own front doors.

The trick is to find ways to keep the flame of passion alight with your partner. Early excitement needs to be replaced by a more sustainable fuel before the flame flickers and dies. But how? Start by soul searching, followed by discussions with your once nearest and dearest.

Long-term love can survive short-term crushes, as long as they're not kept secret. If there's someone you like, tell your partner. It isn't your girlfriend pointing out the other woman's buckteeth and hairy ankles that kills your interest, but the fact that it isn't a private passion.

SWEET TEMPTATION

People and relationships are complex. Working out exactly why you—or, indeed, anyone—does anything is near impossible. There are, however, clues. Good detective work might not lead you to the truth, but what you discover about yourself along the way might be helpful.

So you find yourself thinking obsessively about someone at work. Your "look but don't touch" rule might not have been broken, but there are dangers. You need to ask yourself a number of difficult questions: What is it about this person that has so captivated you? Is it her youth and her ability to make you feel younger/wiser/brighter/funnier/sexier? Are things going on at home that make you feel pushed out, taken for granted, bored or boring, and unheard?

You cannot rule out sheer lust: A new kid on the block, and especially one who makes you feel like a Greek god or cover girl, can have an unsettling effect on you. Likewise changes in circumstances can also rock the boat. A promotion, a new secretary who you see more of than your wife, and opportunities for foreign business trips might put previously undreamed-of temptation in your way and into the equation. These are not excuses and should not be used to justify yourself to anyone, just information to help you understand what's going on between your ears and legs. If you feel you're the only member of the household who washes up, cuts the grass, or takes the kids to judo, and Donna in Accounting takes your mind off these issues, you might have a better idea of how to redirect your frustration.

TEMPTATION DANGER

The daily grind, work stresses, and money problems can all push people away from their partners, making them more likely to succumb to a stranger's seduction.

Comparing your partner unfavorably to your current crush? Rediscover what's so good about him in IDEA 2, *Search for the hero.*

Try another idea . . .

There are times in relationships when eyes (and hands) are more likely to wander:

- After the birth of new baby
- When you're raising a young family
- The so-called midlife crisis
- When the last of your children has left home
- Approaching retirement

In other words, times of change and turbulence. It is hardly surprising that so many people put off confronting these sorts of milestones. Sitting down together, anticipating difficulties, and working out ways around them is a more constructive way forward.

"While the forbidden fruit is said to taste sweeter, it usually spoils faster."
ABIGAIL VAN BUREN, advice columnist

Defining idea . . .

HOW TO AVOID TEMPTATION

Build self-esteem

People often have affairs to feel better about themselves. If you've been laid off, the drudgery at home is only punctuated by arguments about money, and you feel nagged, hooking up with a new partner makes you feel successful at something and desirable again. But only in the short term.

Face problems when they arise

Affairs can be a way of avoiding trouble at home. Relationship difficulties are like weeds: they don't spring up overnight, but, left untended, they can choke and take over. Dealing with the root of small problems as they arise prevents a lot of trouble later.

CULTIVATE EMOTIONAL INTIMACY

Emotional intimacy—developing closeness through expressing feelings—doesn't always come easily. But your partner isn't a mind reader. You both need to say how you feel to understand each other's moods and outbursts. If things feel fiery, take time out to cuddle up.

FORSAKING ALL OTHERS

Affairs can be fun because they are furtive and clandestine. Why not have an affair with your partner? After all, you did it when you were courting. Meet in a bar and pretend not to know each other. Watch other men flirt with her before flirting with her yourself. Wink at him across a crowded train. Have a secret rendezvous. Phone him at work and whisper a playful come-on. Or send risqué e-mails.

Q **I should know better, but I'm crazy about my social work team leader. Other people are beginning to notice. He's married and nothing has happened yet. I know I should change jobs and make things more exciting at home, but after seventeen years, life with Jeff seems so boring. What should I do?**

How did it go?

A *If nothing has happened physically, you're still in a good position to talk to Jeff about your feelings. He might be angry and hurt, but it could jolt him into doing something positive with you about your relationship. One thing's for sure, he'll be a lot angrier if he finds out about your feelings from someone else.*

Q **I'm a surveyor and I can't help flirting with all the hunks I work with. As far as I'm concerned it's all harmless fun, and the guys know it. Unfortunately Paul, my boyfriend, who works on one of the building sites I visit, doesn't agree and is getting increasingly sulky and fed up. Should I try to stop?**

A *Why leave Paul out? Make a point of flirting with him when you visit his workplace. If you carry this through by flirting with him at home, he will find it increasingly hard to think about possible competition.*

79

19

Don't leave me this way

Discovered your partner's using "business trips" to indulge in some extramarital bedroom-business? Caught your girlfriend in flagrante with an older, balder man? If your relationship's shattered by an affair, we'll help you pick up the pieces.

Infidelity erodes intimacy and is a dreadful betrayal. It's also common: even fifty years ago, 60 percent of men and 30 percent of women were unfaithful to their spouses before reaching their fortieth birthday.

The good news? If your partner's been a two-timing treacherous toad, it doesn't have to be the death knell of your relationship. In fact, with hard work and commitment, it can be stronger and better than before, although it may be hard to believe this at the time. These momentous mishaps can motivate you to re-energize your relationship and make each other's happiness top priority, renewing lost closeness. But reconstructing a relationship after an adulterous fallout takes extraordinary dedication and work. It's an old cliché, but you'll need to take life one day at a time and be prepared to ride a wild roller coaster of emotion.

Here's an idea for you...

Screaming, shouting, or beating the cheater to a pulp might make you feel a bit better, but won't repair your relationship. Find some other ways to vent your fury. Write the "other woman" an abusive letter, then tear it up. Go for a swim. Smash some old clay flowerpots.

When you first find out about your partner's sexual infidelity, you'll probably be in shock. This numb feeling may last several days. It's common to feel sick and slightly unreal, as if you're watching yourself perform a part in a play. It doesn't mean you're going crazy; you're stressed out and your mind is doing serious overtime trying to come to terms with the situation. When the numbness wears off, expect waves of anguish and incredulity to hit, knocking you down over and over again each time you manage to get back on your feet. It may take weeks, but eventually you'll start to get angry, not only with your partner but also with yourself, for letting it happen or not noticing sooner.

BABY DON'T GO

The first thing to remember is that you are not alone. Peggy Vaughan, infidelity expert and author of *The Monogamy Myth*, reckons that 60 percent of men and 40 percent of women have an affair at some time during their relationship. And if you're worried your cheating lover will leave, don't panic. Peggy's research discovered that less than 10 percent of people who have affairs divorce and marry their lovers.

Defining idea...

"To handle yourself, use your head; to handle others, use your heart."
ELEANOR ROOSEVELT

SHATTERED DREAMS

In order to rebuild your relationship, you must ask for whatever it is you need to be able to trust your spouse again: time, togetherness, information—or an all-expenses-paid shopping trip to Dubai for you and your best friend. As well as mistrustful, you'll feel suspicious, unsure of yourself, and bitter. You will need to tell your partner what he can do to help. There'll be times when you want to talk and talk about the affair, but we suggest having one evening each week when it just isn't discussed. Unless you spend time as a couple that doesn't revolve around the infidelity, you won't reunite as friends or lovers. Do some relaxing things together that provide pleasure: Take a long bike ride, see a film, or go mini golfing.

FORGIVE

Forgiving is probably the last thing you feel like doing. We understand you want the cheat to squirm in shame indefinitely. But you'll need to absolve him or her before you can both move on. Once you pardon your partner, both the betrayer and betrayed will be able to leave disillusionment and disenchantment behind. So your partner's home late again, with lipstick on his collar and smelling of another woman's perfume? Pluck up the courage to confront him. You can't repair the relationship on your own, without any honesty or commitment from him. It's far better to hear an admission than fear and suspect the worst.

Caught your girlfriend in bed with your granddad and not sure if you can forgive her? Have a look at IDEA 14, *Should I stay or should I go?*

Try another idea . . .

Before you can move on, both of you need to work out what caused the affair. Was it really that she's not getting enough sex at home or is she addicted to the thrill of the chase? Sit down together and read IDEA 29, *Unbreak my heart.*

. . . and another

Defining idea . . .

"*Give yourself three days to take in what has happened. Why three days? Three days is enough time for you to grasp the complexities of what has gone on, to hear what your partner has to say, and for the first element of shock to die down . . . You will also have had two nights of sleep to restore your sense of balance.*"
JULIA COLE, therapist and relationship expert

Q **My boyfriend fessed up to a drunken one-night stand when he was away on business. I have forgiven him, but I can't forget about it. Am I always going to suffer for his wrongdoing?**

A *Some things are impossible to just shrug off and forget. Of course you will always remember it, but in time, see if you can allow it to fade into the background of your relationship.*

Q **My adulterous partner wants to make amends but doesn't know where to start. Do you?**

A *You could start by making him a list.*

20

Culture club

Cupid's arrow can cut through all sorts of social, racial, and religious differences, not to mention gender. Do cultures always have to clash? Of course not. Time to celebrate diversity.

You don't have to be in a mixed-race marriage to experience a clash of cultures. Most couples carry baggage from different backgrounds that only appears long after the honeymoon has set.

ALL BLACK AND WHITE OR SHADES OF BROWN?

Interracial relationships are on the rise. Although they're both Christian, different attitudes and beliefs about birth control methods by Catholic Mary and Protestant Joe caused clashes not apparent in the heady early stages of their affair. We're not just talking about race or ethnicity, but your attitudes, behavior, beliefs and faith, and the way you were brought up.

Here's an idea for you . . .

Cultural difficulties can be overcome if you create some rituals of your own, unique and individual to your relationship. Find ways to celebrate, commiserate, and congratulate. Your own rituals might include lighting candles, dancing to your special songs or music, and eating at a special restaurant.

ROMEO AND JULIET

You're from different families, and families do things differently. Perhaps yours is one of the latter-day Romeo and Juliet romances, where couples fall in love despite the disapproval of families who cannot or will not get along. Being ostracized by two extended families has painful long-term consequences. But is conflict inevitable? We think that cultural hurdles can be overcome and couples who are able to use the resources of two rather than one culture have a better chance of solving problems.

MOSQUES AND MINISKIRTS

Karin, a German Catholic, and Arif, a Muslim born in Burma who grew up in Pakistan, are in a mixed-race marriage that has flourished for over three decades. They met in London as each was adjusting to a third culture: the eccentricities of British life. He shunned a traditional arranged marriage in favor of a beautiful blonde. They were married by an imam in a large mosque in central London. But the bride wore a minidress. Compromise was the hallmark of their early years together, celebrating a fairly Catholic Christmas but observing Islamic bereavement rituals. Karin found it hard at first, but focused on similarities between two seemingly disparate religions. She recognized common rituals and stories. Fairly quickly, they developed a third culture of their own—one where the extended family is important to both of them, but so is an extended wine list.

Guyathri, a Sri Lankan Indian, and her Italian fiancé Fabio have an amazing relationship. We think their secret is that both avoid what anthropologists call "ethnocentrism." This is basically the belief that our own culture is superior to someone else's, or looking at other cultures through our own culture-tinted glasses.

Going through a difficult patch? Take a look at IDEA 13, *Stormy weather*, for ways of weathering the worst of it.

Try another idea . . .

GETTING TO KNOW YOU

Getting to know your partner's culture can be a lifetime's work. Fabio takes the trouble to pronounce Guyathri's name correctly, while all her British friends just call her Kathy. Guyathri has learned Italian, in part to understand Fabio's culture better. She knows it is easy to make assumptions based on the views we're brought up with. Testing these concepts against your partner's experience and knowledge can be eye opening. You probably know bits about your partner's early life, but we suggest you dig a bit deeper. Ask how Jasmine, Johannes, or Jeremiah was brought up; find out about his or her earliest memories of school, and any brothers and sisters. What happened when they were naughty? What was their parents' relationship like? How much does she think yours should be like that? Collect life stories—the more the better—and compare them with your own. What could you gain from your partner's culture? What do you need from your own? Work out where you're willing to compromise and where you're resolute.

Of course you don't need to agree on everything, but it's important to at least agree on what happens at religious festivals and rituals. A shared new culture, unique to the two of you, can transcend differences that

"It's crazy to object to mixed-race relationships.
It enriches our life rather than detracts from it."
ISHI HARBOTT, Tanzanian Muslim and wife of Glenn, a white Briton

Defining idea . . .

87

could otherwise cause separation. Compromise and respect are vital, especially during key life events like the death of a parent or birth of child. What will you do if your Christian wife wants a christening? Working it out beforehand avoids ugly scenes with your in-laws, who'll (probably) take your partner's side.

How did it go?

Q   We're in a mixed-race relationship. One of the drawbacks of living in a small town is that there are a number of racists who make our lives hell when we go out. We love our home and have other good reasons for wanting to stay, but sometimes I worry that all these problems are driving a wedge between us. How can we fight it?

A   *If you allow yourselves to be browbeaten by these racists, they will have won. If you can show that they are not defeating you, they might just leave you alone. Work out what you will do if you are being picked on and recruit whatever help you can. If it's any consolation, you may be making it easier for others in a similar position in the future. They may regard you as pioneers, a couple who, at a local level, broke down racial stereotypes.*

Q   I married young, and converted from Judaism to Islam to make my partner's family happy, but it hasn't worked. I still don't feel accepted by his extended family and mine hasn't forgiven me for leaving my Jewish faith. How can I untangle this mess?

A   *It's always a mistake to join your partner's religion in the belief that it will make things easier. We suggest that you and your partner talk about these difficulties and how they can be resolved. You might find this a difficult subject to broach, but if you avoid it, discontent will fester and you will probably feel increasingly resentful.*

21

I will survive

**Lost a limb or your livelihood, or won the lottery?
Sometimes life shakes your relationship to the core. Here's
how to make the most of those make-or-break times.**

In traditional Jewish wedding ceremonies,
the groom steps on and crushes a glass,
reminding his bride and onlookers of the frailty
of relationships.

You don't have to be Jewish to feel as if your relationship is going to shatter in a
crisis or crack after a series of blows. But instead of letting catastrophes break you
up, we'll show you how to survive, grow closer, and move on.

All couples face occasional crises. Maybe you're mugged on the way home, or
perhaps one day you congratulate yourselves that teenage son Tony hasn't dabbled
in drugs and the next you find out he's dropped out of school and is dealing dope.
Then there are frightening unthinkables that we all hope won't happen to us: death
of a child, being diagnosed with a terminal illness, rape.

THE RAT RACE

In the eighties, psychologist Martin Seligman described how rats adapt to problems
by giving up. The bad news? People aren't so different. In the trade, we call it

Here's an idea for you . . . **It might seem perverse, but why not keep a joint journal during a time of crisis? Writing is a great way of thinking through difficulties and expressing complex feelings.**

"learned helplessness." Basically, this means that when people are confronted by shocks or traumatic events, they adapt by becoming apathetic and helpless. If your partner seems irritatingly numb or cut off after a disaster, it might help to remember that she's responding in the only way she can. The more support, respect, and listening time you provide, the faster she will regain her composure.

FIVE ALIVE

There are five things you can do to strengthen your relationship when disaster strikes:

- Encourage each other. It may sound trite, but little things you can do to make each other feel important, like praising or paying compliments, pay big dividends.
- Make suggestions, give advice, or help each other find answers. It may be deep spiritual comfort or a practical list of helplines and addresses.
- Take a night off. Time away from your troubles doesn't make them go away, but doing fun things and doing your best to be good company takes your mind off your problems for a while.
- Get practical. Address unpaid bills, make funeral arrangements, phone friends and colleagues on your partner's behalf.

Defining idea . . . **"Accept, adapt, and never give up."**
RHONA MACDONALD, GP and medical editor

- Provide emotional support. Even the most inept emotional cripple can provide a bit of basic care, cuddles, comfort, and compassion. Bet you can do it better.

LOVE AND LOSS

We hope you won't ever have to watch a child die, flee a burning building, or rebuild your lives after a war. But death is something we'll all have to face. You don't need a book to tell you that when a friend or relative dies, it's one of the most stressful things you'll go through. It's likely that you and your partner will grieve differently. You might want to talk and cry, she might avoid mentioning it or suddenly idolize her less-than-perfect mother-in-law. These sorts of differences can push a wedge between you, but supporting and accepting each other's reactions will strengthen your relationship as you help each other adapt.

Unemployment is another type of loss that, left unchecked, can eat into the heart of your relationship. Why not use unemployment as a springboard for relationship renewal? Help your partner regain a sense of pride, especially if he's the main or only earner. When Matt was laid off, Elle tried to come up with practical ways to adapt and show flexibility. One of the things she suggested was some horticultural self-sufficiency. Of course, growing vegetables wouldn't feed their family indefinitely, but it reinforced Matt's identity as a provider and gave him a sense of achievement and an outlet for unwanted agitation, as well as something to do. Once Matt got a new job, he remembered how Elle saved him from losing face and their relationship has flourished, much like the weeds in the garden.

Relationship reached breaking point? Take a break. Take her on vacation. Check out IDEA 9, *Vacation romance*, and check in for some R&R.

Try another idea...

"I heard somewhere that a problem at work is like a plane crash that you can walk away from. It's not like your home life where you can't get away from your problems no matter how far you run."
TONY PARSONS, journalist and writer

Defining idea...

91

How did it go?

Q   **My partner was involved in a car accident and the driver in another car was killed. My husband had been drinking, so he's likely to face a prison term. How are we going to cope or face the shame?**

A   *There is no quick answer to this one. Maybe the best you can do is sit down and group the problems into different sections: practical, emotional, social, and so forth. Clearly you will be in for an awful time, and your husband will have to come to terms with the knowledge that he is responsible for another man's death. If you can support each other through this, you will come away from the experience stronger, if sadder, people. You will certainly know who your friends are.*

Q   **Jan, my wife, has diabetes. She has adapted to injecting herself and changing her diet. About a month ago Jan was told she's going blind—which was a real body blow. How can I best help her?**

A   *Small comfort, but the best we can say is that this sort of blindness is progressive so she'll lose her eyesight slowly. This gives you both time to make necessary changes to her lifestyle and your home. You could start to tape outings and family occasions you'd otherwise photograph, to keep audio reminders. We also suggest you give presents that depend on other senses, like perfume. This will be a difficult time, but joining a support group to meet couples in similar predicaments will give you ideas for overcoming the hurdles you face.*

22

Sorry seems to be the hardest word

Some of us would rather face a firing squad than admit we're wrong. If the "s" word sticks in your throat, it's time to bite the bullet.

Everyone screws up sometimes. We all make mistakes, forget important dates, and break promises. But trying to blame our partners makes them feel bad and drags them down to the same level.

The trouble is, deep down you both know you've messed up, and it mangles trust. How do we know? Been there, done that, and learned the hard way that owning up and apologizing helps rebuild damaged trust between lovers.

"I'm sorry." Sounds simple doesn't it? But why do so many of us struggle to say it? Perhaps you are afraid of losing face or looking weak. After all, saying sorry means admitting you're wrong. Perhaps you feel resentful because you always end up apologizing first. It could be that it's not your fault or you don't see eye to eye. It's

Here's an idea for you . . .

Try saying sorry next time you catch yourself hurting your partner's feelings. In your mind, rate how difficult it was out of ten, where ten is "will the ground please open and swallow me up." Your first couple of apologies might feel off the scale, but once you've had a bit of practice, you'll get it down to an easier two or three.

hard to say sorry when you don't know why your partner is angry or upset. Maybe your partner made sarcastic comments when you tried to apologize last time or won't accept your apology, so you wonder what the point is.

WHEN TO SAY SORRY

The best time to say sorry is as soon as you notice that you've hurt your partner. Now, we're not saints either, and know it's incredibly difficult to break mid-argument and offer an apology. Especially if you're winning. If you can express regret after, or even during, an argument, great. On the other hand, it's often preferable to calm down a bit so you don't sound sarcastic or insincere.

HOW TO SAY SORRY

Saying sorry is useless unless your partner knows why you're apologizing. You need to acknowledge what you've done wrong. Be specific. It might make you squirm, but which of these apologies packs the most punch?

"I'm sorry."
"I'm sorry you're upset."
"I'm sorry I upset you by calling you a lazy bum. I didn't mean it. I came home irritable and took it out on you. I know I shouldn't have said it."

Sarcasm or a halfhearted apology, like "You know I didn't mean it," or "You know I'm not all bad," is worse than no apology at all because your partner will probably feel you are being disingenuous.

Sick of saying sorry because you're having the same arguments over and over again? Check out IDEA 13, Stormy weather, for brilliant argument busters.

Try another idea . . .

HOW TO ACCEPT AN APOLOGY

Apologies need to be accepted with grace and goodwill, rather than as ammunition for mudslinging and accusation. "Ha! I knew it was all your fault, you horrid little worm, and now you've accepted it" is a great way not to accept an apology. There are millions of variations of it, but you usually know when you are not accepting an apology properly, as there's really only one right way: "Thank you." So if it's tempting to gloat, remember: you'll probably need to say sorry for something soon yourself.

"You're either part of the problem or you're part of the solution."
ELDRIDGE CLEAVER, founder of the Black Panthers

Defining idea . . .

MORE THAN WORDS . . .

Words are sometimes enough, but actions usually speak louder. This doesn't mean proffering a potted plant or a box of chocolates every time you feel an apology coming on. Gifts can make your partner feel pressured or even blackmailed into accepting your apology before he's ready. If you can't resist saying it with flowers, make sure this isn't the only time you buy your beloved blooms. Far better to follow your verbal apology with action related to your transgression.

"Everyone makes mistakes. To forgive those mistakes is an action of love."
JOHN GRAY, author of *Men are from Mars, Women are from Venus*

Defining idea . . .

If your partner's cross because you never wash the dishes, get the rubber gloves on or buy a dishwasher. If your girlfriend's upset after finding your stash of *Horny Housewife*, cancel the subscription. Whatever you've done, there's no greater crime than apologizing only to commit the same sin again. If you've wounded with words rather than with deeds, action is still called for. When you've said sorry, hold out your hand. Invite your partner to come to you, not to lunge at you.

How did it go?

Q **My girlfriend gets upset with me over small, silly things that most of the time I don't even realize I'm doing. Surely I can't be expected to apologize every other day?**

A *There are a couple of possibilities. Things that seem insignificant to you might be the proverbial last straw for her. On the other hand, blame for all sorts of upsets may be laid at your door. Try acknowledging that she is upset, but don't say sorry right away. Ask her what's made her unhappy, but don't leap in to fix it. Apologize for your misdemeanor, if any, but don't accept liability for all her problems.*

Q **My partner and I get into fights from time to time. I think we're both equally to blame, but it's always me who has to say sorry first before we can put the argument behind us. I'm beginning to resent this, and when I think about it, it makes me angry all over again. Should I confront him with it?**

A *Maybe you should talk to your partner about this—but not during an argument. We know you might worry that it could provoke a quarrel when you are getting along, but this is less damaging that the festering resentment that you seem to be carrying around at the moment.*

23

All by myself

Putting all your emotional eggs in your partner's nest could make it topple over. That doesn't mean you need to find someone else, just the person you've been living with all your life: you.

Hollywood and pop songs brainwash us. Love, they assert, is all you need. Find the girl or boy of your dreams and you'll live happily ever after. What a joke.

If you look to your lover to fill aching gaps in your life you'll inevitably be disappointed in him or her and your relationship. Overdependence and enmeshment breed contempt and self-hatred. A little absence really does make the heart grow fonder. Doing a few things alone makes you a more interesting partner, with more experience and adventures to share when you are together. Think of time apart as fertilizer to cultivate a mature relationship. This way, when you are together, it's out of choice, rather than neediness or dependence.

Find something you love and do it often. It might be going inline skating, performing at a poetry open mic, or having an Indian head massage. Think back to how you enjoyed yourself when you were single. Just because you are in a relationship doesn't mean you have to put away your paintbrushes, ballet slippers, or flute.

AN AIR OF MYSTERY

Develop a side your partner doesn't know or fully understand and they'll become curious and interested. People with an air of mystery, a strong identity, and a range of interests are more attractive. Spend time alone productively and you'll bring skills and knowledge to revive your relationship. Time alone provides space to indulge in activities that don't interest your partner. If you hate football and she hates shopping, why drag a sulking "soul mate" with you to the game or shopping mall?

ALL BY YOURSELF: ONE-NIGHT STANDS

Being the center of someone's universe is initially flattering, but quickly stifling. To give your relationship added vitality, keep a regular night just for yourself. If there's just the two of you, you might be able to have a regular weekday night, but if you've got young children, you'll probably have to eke out a monthly me-date. Your goal is to have fun—be it with friends, trying new activities, or being pampered. So do what you like: beginner's belly dancing, intermediate jam making, or a relaxing aromatherapy massage. But be prepared to explain yourself if your partner comes home early and finds you naked with a Swedish masseuse.

ALL BY YOURSELF: ONCE OR MORE A WEEK

Feeling unfulfilled in your relationship? Easily annoyed, irritable, or resentful? Try making more time for yourself. Whatever they say in the movies, only you can bring what you want into your life. The more needs you can meet yourself, the more likely you are to have lasting love. If you're sick of being a couch potato, get active. And if your partner panics at the prospect of pilates, train for that marathon on your own.

Just because your partner doesn't share your religion doesn't mean you have to ditch your beliefs. You might find attending weekly prayers at the synagogue or going to a lunchtime meditation group strengthens your spirit and nourishes your relationship with a committed atheist. The same is true for politics. If you don't go on an antiwar march because your girlfriend calls it silly, you'll hardly feel at peace with her and might give her her marching orders. Go alone. Her friends or family will probably be delighted to have her to themselves for an afternoon.

The flip side of taking care of number one can be a jealous and resentful partner. If she's begrudging the time you spend without her, check out **IDEA 17, Jealous guy.**

Try another idea . . .

"Taking time to be alone allows a man to feel his independence, self-sufficiency, and autonomy."
JOHN GRAY, psychologist

Defining idea . . .

Defining idea . . .

"Ideally couples need three lives. One for him, one for her, and one for both of them together."
JACQUELINE BISSET, actress

ALL BY YOURSELF: HOME ALONE

You don't have to go out to make the most of your solitude. Being home alone has much going for it. You can fart and not say sorry. You can listen to "your" rather than "our" favorite music and eat what you like, when you like.

Sometimes we love something for the same reasons that our partners hate it. Jill likes *The Sound of Music* because it's sentimental and makes her feel hopeful. Jim hates it because it's sentimental and makes him feel sick. Watching it together doesn't enhance their relationship, but watching the sing-along version on her own makes her more forgiving when he staggers in worse for the wear. When you're home alone, you can gossip on the phone or even book plastic surgery online without worrying about what you partner will think, or soak in a candlelit bath until your skin is blue and wrinkled. Reading with your partner is companionable, but we prefer reading alone: you can rustle newspapers, walk around every few pages to digest a thriller, feel really scared, or laugh out loud.

Q   **I want to spend time reading the newspaper quietly in my study, but my wife keeps interrupting me as she feels left out. How can I tell her she shouldn't?**

How did it go?

A   *Explain that when you are alone it doesn't mean you don't want to be with her, but that you need time to be alone with your hopes, dreams, and newspaper to relax after work and be a better husband.*

Q   **Larry, my partner, is a long-distance truck driver. I knew he would be away from home a lot, but not how empty it would make me feel. I have tried to fill my time with the sort of things that usually interest me, but my attention span when he isn't around is zero. Can you help?**

A   *It sounds to us like you have become overdependent on Larry. Maybe you need to sit down with him and work something out. Rather than hang around waiting for a phone call, you could restrict yourself to phone calls at prearranged times.*

24

Reach out and touch

Words are great, but your fingers can reach places language never can. Here's our eulogy to nonverbal communication and tactile tantalization.

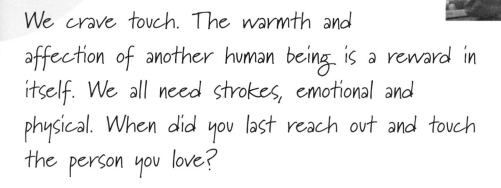

We crave touch. The warmth and affection of another human being is a reward in itself. We all need strokes, emotional and physical. When did you last reach out and touch the person you love?

LET YOUR FINGERS DO THE TALKING

The finest touching is a sensual conversation. When you next touch your partner, wait for a reply before touching further. So if you stroke her cheek, wait until she squeezes your arm before running your finger over her eyebrows. Between people who are attracted to each other, just brushing fingertips can send shock waves. Try making little circles with your fingertips on your partner's palm, inner elbow, or nape of his neck. Do this at mundane times, like waiting for a bus or in the supermarket checkout line. Then next time your partner is waiting for a bus without you, he'll realize that it's just not as much fun as when you're there. A cunning piece of sleight of hand.

Here's an idea for you . . .

Next time you see your partner, touch before speaking. If he's in the kitchen washing dishes, sneak up behind him, slide your hands around his tummy, and cuddle up. When she comes home from work, give her a long hug instead of firing questions or filing complaints.

HUGS

We use hugs to express lots of things, like "hello," "I'm sorry," and "I hope you feel better." Other hugs are good for comforting or making your partner feel warm. Therapist and relationship guru Virginia Satir believes we all need four hugs a day for survival, eight hugs a day for maintenance, and twelve hugs a day for growth. There are three types of hugs, but only one hug hits the spot.

THE QUICKIE

A quick grab and let go, which may be punctuated by a couple of air kisses and *mwah, mwah* noises. This hug's for theatrical types.

THE A-FRAME

Huggers interlock arms and may touch shoulders, but there's no physical contact any lower down. This one's reserved for spinster aunts.

Defining idea . . .

"Touch is important for survival itself. We're meant to be touched. It's part of our inherent genetic development."
ELLIOT GREENE, past president of the American Massage Therapy Association

THE FULL BODY

Wrap your arms around each other, touching from the tops of your heads down to your toes, and bump tummies in the middle. Breathe together, snuggle, and sigh. This one's the real deal.

THE SCIENCE BIT

When nonsexual touch is neglected, we become belligerent and dejected. But why does touch make us feel so good? After prolonged touching, the hypothalamic area of the brain, which controls the fight or flight response, slows down, and your body's natural euphoria-inducing chemicals—endorphins—soar, while the stress hormone cortisol dips. Massage has extra benefits as it promotes deep muscle relaxation. Neck massage has been shown to reduce depression, improve alertness, and help people sleep more soundly. When you're being touched by your beloved, your mind associates all these good feelings with him, leaving you feeling loved and secure. If you're going through a difficult time, try to keep a hand or another part of your body in contact with your beloved. It will help you feel united.

I KNEAD YOU

Hippocrates, the Greek grandfather of medicine, believed daily massage with essential oils was the key to health. We find it unlocks all sorts of sensuous pleasures and possibilities. Massage is a fantastic stress-buster, but it can also excite or invigorate. Before you switch your partner on to massage, switch off your phone. The deeply satisfying sensation is enhanced when the massage oil is heated a little. Immersing a bottle of essential oil in hot water until it reaches body temperature is ideal, but if you haven't got time, warm some oil in your hands first. Chamomile and lavender are said to be calming, whereas ylang ylang is reportedly an aphrodisiac. Once your partner is

Try another idea...

Add music to your massage to touch your partner's emotions as well as his torso. See IDEA 15, *Music, the food of love.*

Defining idea...

"Now that you've given her a luxuriously sensual, stress reducing, lust awakening back massage it's time to whisper seductively in her ear that it's time to roll over . . . "
Advice from CORA EMENS of the New Ancient Sex Academy

relaxed and comfortable, work some oil into his skin. To really bliss your partner out, start with gentle, stroking movements to relax and soothe before applying gentle pressure in places that feel tense or knotted. Change speed every now and then and try moving your hands in little circles, spreading the oil up to the earlobes and down between the toes. Take care not to miss elbows or tickle when you massage foot soles. We suggest you leave punching and chopping to the pros.

How did it go?

Q My husband likes to give me a massage, but he's pretty clueless. His technique seems to be randomly crushing, squeezing, or pounding parts of me. I don't want him to stop—just to stop hurting me. How should I go about it?

A   *Sounds like he needs some lessons. We're not suggesting he rushes out and trains to be a massage therapist, but why not give him a gift certificate for a visit to a professional masseuse (no, not that sort)? With any luck, he'll try out his tricks of the trade on you later. Meanwhile, why not enroll him in a cooking course—he'll be a whiz with dough.*

Q I'm a very tactile sort of person and come from a touchy-feely family. My boyfriend was sent to boarding school, where the only physical contact aside from sex was shaking hands. How can I bring him around?

A   *The short answer is that it's going to take a long time for you to reverse his habits of a lifetime. When you talk about it, avoid those "my family is better than yours" conversations. Instead, gently demonstrate the advantages of what you have. Be sensitive, as he may find touch intrusive, and leave plenty of time for him to enjoy, say, a neck and shoulder massage, before moving on to a full-body massage, which could feel like an invasion.*

25

Taken to task

Projects perk up partnerships. You know what they say: nothing ventured, nothing gained. Relationship reached a stalemate? You might need to reach for the chain saw.

Making log furniture together is just one joint project that can bring back the buzz.

Projects are a vital cog in the relationship re-energizing machine: building a bed, painting a children's ward, making a mosaic mural, training for a marathon, hosting a poetry open mic. Innovative or traditional, it doesn't matter what you do, or even if you succeed. Of course there's a glow as you turn a run-down house into the talk of the town, but the joy is in the journey. When it comes to relationship invigorating schemes, the "shared purpose, vision, and drive" formula is a winner.

POISED FOR ACTION

To the uninitiated, a project with your partner can sound dull. But it is in fact a celebration of what is important to you as well as a platform for showing off the best that your relationship brings out in you. As long as you're both committed, it needn't be a problem if one of you feels more excited about your undertaking than the other. Enthusiasm is infectious. Before long you'll notice your project passion spilling into other areas of your relationship.

Here's an idea for you . . .

Whether you want to start a mixed softball league or co-run a dog-walking group, follow our five-step plan for project perfection:

1. **Think about what you want to achieve together. Maybe you want to focus on creating a relaxing area in the yard.**
2. **What do you need? List practical things, like paint and brushes, as well as imponderables like time.**
3. **Set some deadlines. Twelve trees to be felled before Wednesday.**
4. **Break up your project into manageable tasks. Two trees a day per person.**
5. **Plan some nice stuff to celebrate achievements along the way, as well as the finished project.**

Projects, by their nature, ought to be noncompetitive. Whatever you do, be partners, rather than supervisor and worker. If you decide to make a tapestry wall hanging illustrating your different heritages but your partner has never so much as threaded a needle, be patient and demonstrate how to do it properly. Laughing when she pricks her thumb and bleeds all over the canvas means a fast track to singledom.

Our friend Saima gave up her job as a sari designer when she moved away from India with her husband Rehan, who took up a job as a pediatrician. Unable to find designing work, she felt unhappy in her supportive role and grew resentful of Rehan. They fought daily. She was unhappy and thought of leaving the relationship.

The turning point? Rediscovering a shared talent for calligraphy and turning this into a project making their own Eid cards. They also discovered they have a good eye for color, and are now personalizing their home with throws and soft furnishings.

Want to give your relationship a positive presence in your local community and feel good about what you have together? Shared project ownership says more to your neighborhood about you as a couple than falling out of the same bar every Friday night. For example, instead of feeling bored at home and irritable at the long commute to their nearest theater, movie buffs Piers and Finn started a film club in their local community center. They're treated like a pair of cool culture vultures, and have started to see themselves in that light, too.

Want to set up a soup kitchen for the homeless but your partner scoffs at your lofty, leftie leanings? Let him eat cake. IDEA 23, *All by myself*, shows you how going solo sometimes can strengthen your liaison.

Try another idea...

Like Piers and Finn, taking on a joint venture will help you to cooperate and work together on an instinctive level. Working together toward a common goal develops a couple's communication skills and trust—key skills that improve the most important project of all: your relationship.

"Love does not consist in gazing at each other, but in looking together in the same direction."
ANTOINE DE SAINT-EXUPÉRY, poet, pilot, and philosopher

Defining idea...

How did
it go?

Q **My partner and I started making jewelry together as a hobby. For the first couple of years it was fun. Recently I've started to feel there's nothing else in our relationship. We spend weekends at bead fairs, evenings at advanced macramé classes, and at night there's even beading in the bedroom. If we go out, we end up talking about new designs. Our beading has taken over the apartment. How do we stop it from taking over our lives?**

A *Sounds like a small industry. Yours are the sorts of problems common in couples who live and work together. Ban beading one night a week, and hopefully it won't be just your gems that sparkle.*

Q **We'd like to have a joint project but are saving up to move in together. Is there anything we can do that won't cost a lot?**

A *We were broke when we first moved in together and couldn't afford any new furniture. Instead of letting it get us down, we made a bed out of pallet boards, found a leather chair at a yard sale, and lived like bohemians in an attic. It wasn't the most comfortable time in our life together, but it was fun and gave us lots of memories that keep our love alive.*

Q **My boyfriend and I have recently taken on an overgrown area that we want to make into an organic garden. Trouble is, he's very competitive, always pointing out what he does better. How will this enhance our relationship?**

A *You can't change him, but you can change the rules so that you compete as a team. So instead of seeing who can weed fastest, see if you can weed three beds together before the cocktail hour. Once he realizes that you can achieve much more together than alone, he'll always be on your side.*

26

Let's face the music and dance

Tango or twist, salsa or samba, if you're missing romance, it's time to dance. There may be troubles ahead, but in your dancing shoes you can quick-step away from them.

Dancing is sexy, sassy, and keeps you fit for life and love. When you and your partner move to a groove, you'll have fun and feel great about your relationship. Take your partners, please.

FIRST TANGO IN PHILLY?

Perhaps the most erotically charged moment of any film we've seen was the dance sequence in *Scent of a Woman*. Al Pacino plays a blind man who meets a young woman impatiently waiting for her partner in a ballroom. Pacino, having asked if he can sit next to her to "protect her from the womanizers," asks her for a dance when the band strikes up the opening chords of a tango. There follows a few minutes of filmic bliss as Pacino expertly cavorts his partner around an empty dance floor. Passion and raw sexuality are hinted at behind the dance's formal façade. The result is magical. The music stops and he escorts her back to the table. Everything and nothing has happened.

Roll up the rug and practice your moves at home. To add verve and vitality to your repertoire, there's nothing like being inspired by peppy pros. Why not rent a DVD with a difference? They can take you from beginners to pros in capoeira, street jazz, or flamenco. Or, if you prefer, kick off with a can-can, take in a slick show dance, or be moved by the grace and poise of a Bolshoi ballet.

MAY I HAVE THE PLEASURE OF THIS DANCE?

Okay, that was film and this is life. Maybe you're not Al Pacino and your local dance school isn't some swanky New York hotel. However, the people who devised ballroom dances knew a thing or two about us mortals and our dreams. Dancing—this sort, anyway—is about the power of suggestion and understated elegance, masterful holding, tender touching, and moving to the rhythm of sensuous music. Dancing is a skill all couples should share for life. Choreographically naive? A few lessons at a local dance class are all you need to twirl your lover and your relationship around.

For the duration of a waltz or quickstep, Joe and Josephine Average can be transported, lost in a bubble of bliss, up there with Fred and Ginger. As near to heaven as you can get away from a bedroom.

STILL NOT CONVINCED?

Let's talk about clothes. Men look magnificent in a dinner suit or tuxedo. They are, after all, designed to minimize sagging shoulders and stomachs. Well-cut ball gowns make the most of what a woman has and conceals what she hasn't. Dressing for the ball gives back the luster to most tarnished relationships.

POP CULTURE

Ready to concentrate on some intense routines? Try jazz dance. Don't be confused by the name— this isn't all Duke Ellington and Count Basie. Although these moves were originally inspired by jazz and musical theater, this is really club-dancing. If there's no class close to home, have a fun night in copying dancers from your favorite video or switch on a music video channel. If you're looking for something hotter and fiery, Latin moves like the samba, salsa, cha-cha, lambada, and rumba are often taught in bars and clubs.

TAP TO IT

Before you titter at tap dancing, forget prissy little girls stamping shiny shoes or octogenarians doing Irish jigs and spare a thought for Fred Astaire and Gene Kelly. Some elegance from the forties can fortify your relationship.

LET IT ALL HANG OUT

Perhaps you'd prefer the raw physicality of hip-hop, fusion funk, or zoonation? Whatever your style, dancing doesn't have to be stuffy. Belly dancing is the oldest dance form in the world—more sensually evocative than erotically provocative, and not a flat stomach in sight.

Going to the ball, dance hall or nightclub? Cinderella had a fairy godmother to make her look like a million dollars, but you have IDEA 34, *You look wonderful tonight.*

Try another idea . . .

"Dancing is a perpendicular expression of a horizontal desire."
GEORGE BERNARD SHAW

Defining idea . . .

"Will you won't you, will you won't you, will you join the dance?"
From *Alice in Wonderland* by LEWIS CARROLL

Defining idea . . .

113

Q   **We'd like to take up dancing but there are so many different
types, we don't know where to start. How did you go about it?**

A   *Actually, we went for a sampler session in a large dance studio where you
can wander around and look through huge plateglass windows at classes in
forms of dancing you have never heard of. You can learn to dance like
Michael Jackson, line dance, contemporary ballet, samba, and a great deal
more. When making your choice, all sorts of things need to be factored in:
whether you could use it away from the school, your gut feelings about a
particular teacher and other class members, and how easy it would be to
get there. Discuss the pros and cons, or flip a coin and go for it.*

Q   **I really want to be able to do a few basic dances because we go to
the occasional dinner-dance and it would be nice to waltz and
quick-step. I've been to ballroom classes over the years, but I'm
hopeless: My legs refuse to do what my mind and teachers tell
them to do. It's so humiliating; my wife is quite good but I always
feel I'm holding the rest of the class up. How can I hold my own?**

A   *We understand; don't you just hate those naturals who pick it up so
effortlessly? Why not book a few secret private lessons and learn at your
own pace? Wouldn't it be great to crack it and expertly lead your wife
through a waltz the next time you are out at a dinner-dance?*

27

Dump your junk

It's not just fat that most of us acquire as we grow older, it's possessions, too. Clear out the clutter and make room for love.

How will sifting through the contents of the spare bedroom improve your relationship? Aren't there better ways of spending time together? We'll show how sorting, saving, storing, or selling saves relationships.

Clutter costs you and your relationship more than you can afford. Do you like to keep stuff? Is your home disorganized? Like poison ivy, clutter takes over, obscuring and stifling. Untidiness makes us frustrated and puts stress on relationships. It's also a massive time waster. It'll sap your passion and drain away intimacy. But we're no minimalists. Where would we be without the lawn mower, electric drill, bread maker, or computer? Problems come when we hang on to so much clutter that we can't find things we need, don't feel we have room to move, and waste hours each week trying to find things.

Here's an idea for you . . .

Enjoy yourselves as you get organized. We love to put on our favorite tunes and dance in newly created space. Find out more in IDEA 26, *Let's face the music and dance.*

Laura and Jean-Claude used to spend about twenty minutes each morning hunting for the house and car keys before heading off to work, each minute increasing the likelihood of getting snared in traffic. They started their days tense and sniping, and that was the good bit. A key hook changed their lives.

Jake works while Katherine is a full-time homemaker. You don't have to spend too much time in their home before overhearing remarks like, "Why do you always hide my planner?" and charged questions like, "Where did you put my shoes this time?" By itself, each question may be small, but each is a little brick. Over time, the bricks will build up into a wall that will prevent good communication and goodwill from getting through. Find a home for the planner and invest in a shoe rack, and walls like these will never be built.

Rolling up your sleeves and sorting out your attic, cellar, apartment, shed, or garage probably isn't your idea of spending quality time together. We'd all like some little elves to visit at night and rummage through that pile of lecture notes, go through those cans of wall paint, or sift through the records, weeding out the albums you know you'll never listen to again.

Defining idea . . .

"People are important, not things. We have made our stuff more important in our lives than our relationships with others. When we keep that perspective, it is easier to change."
MIKE NELSON, author

What, no elves? You need four big receptacles—garbage bags, boxes, shopping carts, or whatever you have handy. Label them: garbage, recycling, charity, and repair. As you sort through your stuff, either put it away, find a home for it, or toss it into one of these containers. Save oodles of time by only touching each item once. You can confer; indeed, we'd urge you to ask your partner what he wants done with his tennis racquet. If he has to buy it back from the charity store, it might put the wrong sort of bounce back into your relationship.

Now your bedroom is spic-and-span, have fun turning it into a love temple. See IDEA 33, Bedroom eyes.

Try another idea . . .

As you peruse your bits and pieces, you're bound to be reminded about old times together. By all means reminisce and share your happy memories, but don't hang on to that old poster-size photo of your ex-husband for so-called sentimental reasons. Letting go of souvenirs from botched relationships frees you from the past and helps you focus on each other. Save the family silver though. Heirlooms and valuables are sacred.

TURN YOUR CLUTTER INTO CASH

Turn unwanted clutter into cash by holding an online auction or taking part in a yard sale. Instead of saving the proceeds, why not reward your efforts and enjoy a night out together, celebrating your tidy home.

Feeling overwhelmed with the thought of clearing all your clutter? How about starting with just a drawer? It doesn't matter if it's where you store your socks or your stationery, just make a start. Once you've decluttered that first drawer, a chest of drawers, closet, or bedroom are within reach.

Defining idea . . .

"*In relationships, most women become slaves to men because men know women won't put up with a mess. If you treat your husband like someone you just happen to live with, it will put you both on equal ground. It will also make him realize he has responsibilities and should be respectful of the person he's living with. Tell him he's got to do his share of tidying and you won't do it for him.*"
PHILLIP HODSON, psychotherapist and relationship expert

How did it go?

Q **We've got a tidy and organized apartment and our relationship is the better for it. Trouble is, every day we get a massive onslaught of paper in the mailbox. Some of it is junk, but not all. How can we keep on top of it?**

A *To get rid of junk mail, get yourselves taken off mass-mailing lists. Sign up for the National Do Not Mail List at www.directmail.com/junk_mail/. Also we've found that opening our mail next to a wastepaper basket has been a massive help. Once we've read it, it's filed or recycled. Many couples make it a rule never to pick up a piece of paper twice. The natural tendency is to read things and put them away to attend to later. But when later comes, those pieces of paper have turned into a massive pile.*

Q **I'd love to unclutter our place. I've been trying for years. Unfortunately I'm married to a hoarder. He brings in new stuff quicker than I can get rid of the old. How can I win?**

A *Maybe you could introduce a couple of clutter-free zones into your place. Put all his junk into a couple of containers and offer to help sort it out. Rattling a box of matches near them will get his full attention.*

118

28

Hike up the heartbeart

Daredevil dates that make your partner's heart beat faster will make you irresistible. Hike up his heartbeat and reap the results.

Turbo-charging your relationship isn't about red roses, scented candles, or vintage champagne. Sharing a breathtaking adrenaline rush with your partner will give her the hots for you all over again.

YOU MAKE MY HEART BEAT FASTER

There was an important study in the sixties that looked at men's attraction to women. Scientists asked a group of guys to rate the attractiveness of photos of nude women while listening to what they believed to be their own heartbeats. It was in fact a prerecording. As their "heartbeat" increased, guys scored the women as more attractive. They reckoned, if their heart was beating faster, they must be turned on by the photos. You can exploit this study to improve your relationship. We're not suggesting you pipe heartbeat music around your home, but that you hike up your partner's heartbeat. How? When we're scared, we produce extra adrenaline. It's called the fight or flight chemical because of the effects it has on our bodies. Most importantly, it hikes up the heart rate.

Here's an idea for you . . .

For an unbeatable combination of adrenaline and fun, why not visit a theme park? Hurtle full speed down water rides or roller coasters. Don't be put off by hordes of noisy schoolkids by avoiding weekends and the school holidays. Many theme parks are open late one evening a week. Find out if yours is and go on a late date with a difference.

BRIDGING THE GAP

Thirty years ago, a couple of psychologists wrote a paper titled "Some evidence for heightened sexual attraction under conditions of high anxiety." This is what they did: They asked a group of guys to cross one of two bridges. The first was a scarily shaky suspension bridge far above a canyon; the other was a solid bridge just a short height over a small brook.

After each man crossed his allocated bridge, he was met by a beautiful researcher. She asked him to complete a short questionnaire, in which he had to categorize some fairly vague pictures of people. When he'd done this, the beautiful researcher gave the guy her phone number. "Call me," she said, "if there's anything you want to ask about the study."

Guess what? The guys who crossed the wobbly bridge were much more likely to call. What's more, they found more sexy themes in the ambiguous pictures they were shown after crossing the bridge. Why? Well, crossing the suspension bridge gave them an adrenaline surge and hiked up their heartbeats. When they saw the beautiful woman, the men misinterpreted their increased heart rates and thought they must be sexually aroused. Do something scary with your beloved, and make it work for you.

Not sure? The bad news is that the converse works, too. If you and your partner are supremely bored, sooner or later she'll start to think of you as dramatically boring. Enough theory. What are you waiting for? Go on a different sort of date. We dare you to try one of these:

So you've bungee jumped and skydived and your pulses and passions are soaring. Why not have a wet and wild underwater adventure? Turn to IDEA 40, *How deep is the ocean?*, and take the plunge.

Try another idea . . .

Parasailing

We're not suggesting you take your partner for a walk on a wobbly bridge over a gaping canyon, but parasailing re-creates the scenario pretty well. Next time you're at the sea, instead of lying on the beach, go gliding. Hold on to each other tight, and when you're high above the water, whisper "I can really feel your heart beating quickly."

Bungee jumping

Get your partner to jump first and look deep into his eyes before he drops into the deep. Better still, find a center that does couple bungees, where you jump on the same cord.

"To mistrust science and deny the validity of the scientific method is to resign your job as a human. You'd better go look for work as a plant or wild animal."
P. J. O'ROURKE

Defining idea . . .

"The pattern of autonomic arousal does not seem to differ from one state to another. For example, while anger makes our hearts beat faster, so does the sight of a loved one."
WALTER CANNON, physiologist and emotion expert

Mountain biking

Speed junkies will love an exhilarating off-road tour across rough terrain, along mud roads, down hills, and across creeks.

Whitewater rafting

Thrills and spills guaranteed to pump your love muscle to the max. Plus it'll build team spirit as you work together to control the raft.

Jet Skiing

Another date that'll build a stronger partnership as you navigate rivers at soaring speeds and do 360 degree turns. Hold on tight.

And yes, we sound like your mother, but please be careful on your daredevil dates. Remember, you're aiming to raise adrenaline levels, not the mortality rate.

Q   I'm terrified by the thought of any of your daredevil dates. My husband would probably be up for most of them, but I'd just wimp out at the last minute. Actually, I'm in a bit of a funk just thinking about it. How can I overcome my fear?

How did it go?

A   *No need to worry. Remember the beautiful researcher? She didn't actually cross the bridge with the guys. Why not give your partner a present with added thrill factor, like a flying lesson or skydiving, and be there to meet him at the bottom? He'll associate you with his hair-raising adventure so you'll get all the benefits.*

Q   My girlfriend is recuperating after a motorcycle accident so extreme sports are out of the question. We've been bored and bickering. Any ideas?

A   *Why not rev up the fear factor by renting a scary film? Watch it late with the lights off for added vim and vigor.*

29

Unbreak my heart

So you've done the dirty: been caught with your skirt up or pants down. Time to face the music or face the judge.

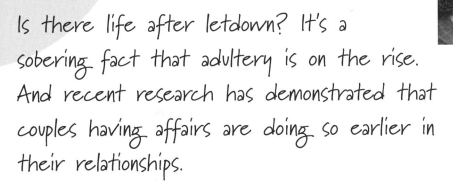

Is there life after letdown? It's a sobering fact that adultery is on the rise. And recent research has demonstrated that couples having affairs are doing so earlier in their relationships.

Before 1960, men who played away waited on average eleven years before doing the dirty; after 1970, they could last only five. With women, the figures are even more dramatic: before 1960, those who dallied with the proverbial postman did so on average fourteen years after saying "I do." Yet after 1970 they had overtaken adulterous men and were cheating a whole decade earlier. Of course, many remained faithful (or lied to the pollsters), but this research confirms observations that there is more temptation out there and more people willing to bend their vows.

WHAT DO YOU DO IF YOU ARE ONE OF THEM?

Psychotherapist and relationship expert Jonathan Robinson suggests a four-step approach to rebuilding broken trust. He's given it the mnemonic RARE, which stands for:

Here's an idea for you . . .

Why not leave the kids with Granny, go away for the weekend, and work your way through the RARE steps in a hotel?

Defining idea . . .

"I didn't know why I had done this to Martha, broke her heart. I mean, what was I doing walking away from my wife and my past and myself? Maybe I was temporarily insane or chemically imbalanced, or this was an inevitable, if unflattering, craving for sexual variety—a genetic command, simple as that. I didn't believe any of this, but didn't want to believe either that I was capable of battering Martha with infidelity, of abandoning her to panic and depression, of behaving like some jaded libertine. I was a stranger to myself."
JOHN DEFRESNE, author and teacher

RESPONSIBILITY

In essence, if you've cheated, you have to take responsibility. Blaming a leggy pole dancer for leading you on doesn't cut it. If you refuse to be accountable for your own actions, it's harder for your partner to trust you again.

AN APOLOGY

Yes, you've guessed it. You owe your partner an unreserved apology for a number of things: breach of trust, hurt, humiliation, the way she found out, and the blow to her self-esteem.

REQUEST INFORMATION

Ask your partner what he needs to feel better. Some want to be held, others want to be left on their own for a few days. It's likely that your partner will want to know many—possibly all—gory details. Men usually want to know what actually happened, while women are also likely to need to know why it happened. And you are going to have to talk and talk and talk. You might be bombarded with questions for hours, days, or even weeks. This is the price to pay for cheating.

ENTRUST

According to Robinson, when a bond is broken a new one has to be made before trust can be rebuilt. It's time to make a new promise and stick to it. "I won't ever speak to the trapeze artist again" may be a good start.

THEN WHAT?

So that's the theory; now you need to put it into practice. You and your partner need to establish why the affair happened. What's gone from your relationship to leave room for adultery? Have your conversations become mundane or as exciting as leftover soup? If so, you could both do with developing your own interests. Perhaps foibles and quirks in your partner that once seemed so delightful are now a source of irritation. Maybe sex has become as much fun as brushing your teeth? It might be that the "guilty party" is feeling marginalized after the birth of a baby. People sometimes stray because they've felt isolated or misunderstood, and the affair provides a temporary replacement of depleted self-esteem. In short, there may be a thousand potential difficulties in your relationship that need to be addressed. But it doesn't get you off the hook. We know you won't thank us for saying it, but having a fling rather than facing your problems says a lot more about you than it does about your partner or the person you had an affair with. And if you are trying to escape from something that feels awful, it's time to stop running and face up.

But it's not all bad news. Many couples who have reached the precipice have managed to turn back and sort things out, and as a result have a stronger, deeper love.

Maybe you have said sorry and the message hasn't gotten through, or you need other ways of expressing yourself. IDEA 22, *Sorry seems to be the hardest word*, is teeming with great suggestions.

Try another idea...

"He who excuses himself, accuses himself."
GABRIEL MEURIER, Flemish philologist

Defining idea...

127

How did it go?

Q **My wife found out that I had been seeing a young colleague outside work. I ended the affair and told my wife everything, but she's still not satisfied. Things seem to get better, then she starts interrogating me again—sometimes all night! How can I get her to stop?**

A *Try seeing it from her perspective. Your wife wants to understand why it happened. Asking endless questions is her way of making sense of a horrible shock and betrayal. We suggest you write her a letter that answers all her questions. You could use the RARE formula. Other couples have negotiated a time to talk each week and veto conversations about the affair after bedtime.*

Q **I went out on a girls' night with a bunch of women from work. We all had too much to drink and I ended up with this guy and spent the night at his place. My husband found out and was hurt and upset. I've said I'm sorry and he said it was okay, but it isn't. That was three months ago, and he's still cold with me. Nothing I do to make it better seems to work. What should I try next?**

A *Three months might seem a long enough time to you, but it can often take a lot longer. You need to just keep battling on, and when opportunities come up to talk about it, continue to eat that humble pie.*

30

Our house

Mad about mulch? Fretting over fencing? Arguing about awnings? The foundations of your miscommunications may be closer to home than you think.

Is it time to clear out and cuddle up?
Or should you move out and move on?

We all know how it feels to see dirty dishes left in the sink again, or to see the bedroom floor used as a laundry basket. Our homes affect how we feel about our relationships.

HOUSEHOLD HEARTSINKS

Re-wallpapering your hall for the third time? Hacking back the ever-encroaching weeds in your oversized garden for the ninth consecutive weekend? If all your time, energy, and money are being poured into your bricks and mortar, it's not surprising your relationship needs re-cementing.

JUNK JUNKIES

We've yet to meet a natural minimalist. Everyone picks up clutter along the way. But often, treasures from our past anchor us there, preventing us from concentrating on what matters now. If the thought of parting with old books, music,

Here's an idea for you . . .

Some homes, and couples, have a mass-produced feel. We don't have to live like that. Try to devote one part of your home to your relationship and romance. This will usually be the bedroom, but if you live in a studio, sleeping on a fold-away futon, you might have to use a bit of imagination. It doesn't have to be all pink hearts and fat cherubs in fluffy clouds. Move the exercise bike and television, hang a couple of pictures of the two of you, a framed poem, soft lighting– whatever makes your hearts beat faster.

and clothes you've grown out of depresses you, at least sell, donate, or throw away reminders of previous relationships. When John moved in with Marie, he felt uncomfortable in the home she shared with her ex-husband Geoff. It was ages before they could afford to move to a new place, but, remembers John, "The relationship changed for the better when we threw out their old bed and bought a new one."

SPACE INVADERS

When one partner moves into a home the other already owns or rents, it's vital to make space. "I don't feel like I fit into Lynne's life," complained Bertie, who has lived with Lynne for three years. "The bathroom cabinet is crammed full of her stuff, and there's nowhere in the closet for my suits." Their relationship felt "a lot more equal" after Lynne went through the apartment, clearing out old books and CDs, and "rationalizing" her vast collection of near-identical red lipsticks.

IS BIG BEAUTIFUL?

Some couples work so hard climbing the property ladder that it destroys their lives and relationship. A large house, ideal for a growing family (and growing cabbages), might become a white elephant when the kids have left. Attractions like walking distance to school or a workplace, or the need to be near parents, are redundant if the kids are at college, you've retired, and your parents are dead. Rather than being your greatest asset, your home might be asset-stripping your love life.

Time to move out and move on? Ponder these questions with your beloved:

- What does this home stop us from doing?
- What was it that first attracted us to this home?
- How have our needs and circumstances changed since?
- How has the area changed? Is it a better or worse place than it was?
- Could we convert the house and change its use?
- What would we miss if we moved?
- If we replaced this house with an inexpensive apartment, how would we spend the windfall?

Harry and Jasmine did this exercise and discovered that Harry had fallen out of love with gardening. During summer evenings the need to water hundreds of prize squash had restricted vacations to rare weekend breaks. Their house was ideal for entertaining, but once they realized it had been eight years since their last dinner party, they thought, so what? They took French lessons and moved to Provence, where they are now happy running a small gîte.

So your new pared-down home has freed up some time? Check out IDEA 28, *Hike up the heartbeat*, for some tips on how to make your spare time sensational.

Try another idea...

"I really do believe it: if you can live through remodeling a home, you can live the rest of your lives together."
JENNIFER ANISTON

Defining idea...

131

Inge and Klaus came to a different conclusion. Their house was also too big. Bedrooms belonging to their grown-up children had become shrines to their teenage years and other rooms were only used to store clutter. They decided to take in students from the local college and were astonished at the money it brought in. "We were worried at first," confided Inge, "but the students have been great. It's kept us young and they've introduced us to new things like comedy clubs and Egyptian dancing. We should have done this years ago."

APARTMENT DWELLERS HAVE MORE FUN

So think Ted and Diandra. "We've done the suburban commuter thing," explained Ted. "It suited us then, but now we have a different life."

"Moving to the city is the best thing that ever happened to us," chips in Diandra. "There is so much to do. I couldn't believe how many evening classes we can get to by train. We both love jazz, so we go to clubs at the beginning of the week when it's cheaper and can walk home along the river afterward. It's like a second courtship."

NOMADS ARE US

E-mail and cell phones have freed many couples from the need to keep a house and a fixed address. RVs and a life on the road have replaced lawn cutting and card nights.

Q   Isn't moving one of the most stressful things that can happen to you, up there with divorce, death, and end-of-season play-offs? That can't be good for our relationship. We've toyed with thoughts of moving for ages, but are worried that it'll be a mistake and we'll come to regret it. Will we?

How did it go?

A   *You might, but life is risky. Clinging on to what you have won't guarantee you happiness either.*

Q   We have moved to a big family home from an apartment. We can only just afford the mortgage. How can we furnish all those extra rooms?

A   *The answer may be in your local thrift shops. You can pick up secondhand chairs cheaply, and if you let friends and colleagues know that you have space to fill, before too long you'll be bombarded with castoffs. You could paint wooden floors until you have money for carpets, and buy cheap material and make curtains yourselves. Pallets you find at building sites make excellent bases for beds, and the cardboard boxes that freezers come in can be converted into dining room tables.*

31

Gym'll fix it

So the get up and go has gotten up and gone. Flab has replaced what was once firm. More jiggle than gigolo? Time to ease yourselves back to exercise.

If the mere thought of exercise makes you sweat, think of the bedroom benefits. Look in the mirror: Are you going to grin and hide it or slim and bare it?

The endorphin rush you get from exercise can beat your relationship blues.

WORK IT, BABY

Exercise is a first-rate stress buster, one that gives you extra energy at the end of the day. You probably already know that exercise releases endorphins—natural feel-good hormones—into our brains. But did you know a workout can do wonders for a flagging libido? Exercise and you'll have better circulation, sending blood to those important places more efficiently. Reducing your body fat helps sustain a higher sex drive. Working out with your partner also helps you to motivate each other and reach goals that seem elusive when you're doing it alone.

Here's an idea for you . . . **Feeling unfit? Building your fitness with a gentle stroll together can benefit your relationship in other ways. Check out IDEA 3, A walk on the wild side.** .

How does exercise help grease the old love machine? For starters, it opens clogged arteries. It's no secret that high cholesterol blocks arteries, narrowing them. What a lot of guys don't realize is that this happens in penile arteries, too. When it does, it causes erection problems.

LET'S GET PHYSICAL

A study published in the *Archives of Sexual Behavior* described how seventy-eight sedentary but healthy men took part in moderate aerobic exercise, three to four days a week for nine months. They reported significant increases in sexual arousal, activity, function, and satisfaction. They had sex 30 percent more frequently than before, whereas the sex lives of a control group stayed the same.

Defining idea . . . **"Exercise ferments the humors, casts them into their proper channels, throws off redundancies, and helps nature in those secret distributions, without which the body cannot subsist in its vigor, nor the soul act with cheerfulness."**
JOSEPH ADDISON, English essayist, poet, and politician

Another recent research study looked at three groups of couples. The group that did energetic sports, like bungee jumping and white-water rafting, showed greater improvements in rekindling intimacy and interest in sex.

"We've been making out a lot more since we started working out," Lola told us. Lola and Len started running and swimming together after Len had a heart attack and have been surprised to find each other extra-desirable. At its most basic, sex is an aerobic activity, so boosting cardiovascular fitness by walking, running, cycling, or swimming for at least twenty minutes a day is a great way to practice in public.

ADD MUSCLE TO YOUR LOVE LIFE

Researchers at the University of California discovered that after an hour's exercise three times a week, men had sex more often and found it more satisfying. It's not just guys, either. Women who worked out had sex more frequently and enjoyed it more than their couch potato contemporaries. Scientists at the University of Texas studied thirty-five young women. They asked them to watch two films on two different occasions. The first film was a short travelogue, the second was X-rated. The first time, women cycled hard for twenty minutes before watching the films. The second time they didn't. Researchers calculated their sexual response using a device that measures blood flow in genital tissue, and discovered that the women's vaginal responses were 169 percent greater after exercising. Whether the travelogue had any effect is unclear.

Dancing can be magnificent exercise. Read IDEA 26, *Let's face the music and dance*, to find out how dance can rejuvenate other unfit areas of your love life, too.

Try another idea . . .

"To resist the frigidity of old age, one must combine the body, the mind, and the heart. And to keep these in parallel vigor one must exercise."
BONSTETTIN

Defining idea . . .

"The physically fit can enjoy their vices."
LORD PERCIVALL

Defining idea . . .

TONE UP

We know lifting all those weights is boring, but how's this for a motivator? Improving your muscle tone enhances orgasms. And toned bodies are also better at holding new positions for longer. Regular strength training gives you a sexier body and raises testosterone. And you know what that means.

We realize not everyone's a gym bunny. Would you prefer to glide around an ice rink? By all means ditch your Lycra leotard, but include a couple of races to get the heart rate up and rev up your love interest. Instead of sitting on a bench, play Frisbee in the park. Or buddy up with some other couples and go bowling. Form a team with your partner or play guys against girls.

How did it go?

Q **I've recently been in training for a triathlon, and sex has been the last thing on my mind. All this exercise seems to be having the opposite effect with me. Am I weird?**

A *Oops. We haven't mentioned that hard training has been linked to a decrease in sex drive. There are a few possible reasons: low testosterone or irritation to your prostate gland caused by friction when you've been running. Overtraining can also wreak havoc on your immune system, which can have negative effects on sexual performance. Take a break from training and enjoy a couple of nights in.*

Q **My husband and I loved running together, but he's had to stop because of knee problems. We've been swimming, but just doing laps up and down is so tedious. What other low-impact activity would you suggest?**

A *It's difficult when injuries jeopardize routines, but try to see it as an opportunity to try something completely different. If water aerobics seems too frumpy, why not have a go at water polo?*

32

April in Paris

Long-haul lovers know mini-vacations make a massive difference. Whether it's to Paris in the springtime or New York in the fall, whisk your partner away before she falls for somebody else.

Make—or break?

Been there, done that? Sorry. Just because you went away for a dirty weekend during your first month together doesn't mean you never go again. Mini-vacations are a chance to live life away from the mundane grind. Forty-eight hours to put some sparkle back and see you through hard times. But beware. A bad mini-vacation can herald a major breakdown in stale relationships.

People run into trouble when they think it's all location, location, location. It doesn't matter whether you go to Paris or Poughkeepsie; it's what you do when you get there.

The good news? Organizing a romantic mini-vacation is a piece of cake when you know how. The secret is to forget all about location and instead plan around an activity your partner will delight in. Bed-and-breakfasts with four-poster beds are all very well, but unless you plan what to do when you get there, you could end up bored and arguing.

Does your partner have an unfulfilled ambition? If she's always wanted to fly and you take her on a crash course, she'll have her head in the clouds over you. Or is there a place that holds special memories for you both—the place where you went

Here's an idea for you . . .

Next time your partner enthuses about something, see if you can plan a break around it. So if he's bopping around the kitchen to the Red Hot Chili Peppers, buy a pair of out-of-town tickets and make a surprise weekend of it.

on your honeymoon, or the town where you first met? Has your boyfriend got a hobby that you could take part in for a weekend? Why just watch him shoot clay pigeons? Grab a gun and go for it together. Book readings, music recitals, cooking classes, a night at the theater—even naked outdoor Tae Kwon Do— plan your break around his favorite activity and then go and book the tickets (preferably to somewhere warm).

When your chocoholic chap realizes you've taken him to Belgium for a handmade truffle demonstration, or your wife realizes you've traveled miles away to see her favorite comedienne, it all falls into place. When the world revolves around you for a couple of days, you feel understood, loved, and cherished. We're not saying four-poster beds, champagne, and roses don't help; they're just optional extras. Think of them as garnish.

If you can keep your mini-vacation secret from your partner and make it a surprise, you're on to a winner. When Jess was stressed at work, Tom dropped their children off at his mother's, packed two overnight bags, and collected Jess from the office one Friday. They had two nights in a spa, where Jess was pampered, and they both rode horses, which they hadn't done since starting their family. When they returned, Tom's mother commented that they looked like honeymooners.
If you can't collect your partner, you could send a taxi, stretch limo, rickshaw, or a first-class train ticket in a bunch of roses. A mysterious e-mail saying "Meet me at the airport at 7 p.m." will make your beloved's heart beat faster.

WITHOUT BREAKING THE BANK

If money is tight, we suggest you spend most of it on your activity and scrimp on the accommodation. You can turn a shabby room in a cheap B&B into a boudoir in six simple steps.

- Arrive before your partner if you can, and collect her from the station once you've set the room up. If you've driven down together, drop her off to look at shops or a landmark, or to eat cake, anything, while you glam up the room.
- If the bedsheets are nylon or chintzy, strip 'em off. Replace them with the plain white cotton pillowcases and sheets that you've cunningly secreted about your person (or bought at the local store).
- You need two roses and a jar. Put the healthier looking rose in the jar of water and put it on your partner's side of the bed. Scatter the petals of the other rose over the crisp white sheets.
- Chill a bottle of bubbly in the landlady's fridge, in your sink, or by dangling it out of the window—whatever. It doesn't even have to be "proper" champagne—any sparkling wine will do. Effort and atmosphere impress more than big bucks. You can buy inexpensive disposable champagne flutes wherever picnic stuff is sold. Put a couple of flutes on your partner's side of the bed and put a few rose petals around the bases.

Can't get a weekend off together for several months? Have some great days together in the meantime. See IDEA 37, What a difference a day makes.

Try another idea . . .

"After sitting in semi-darkness for third weekend running with Daniel's hand down my bra, fiddling with my nipple as if it were some sort of worry bead, I suddenly blurted out, 'Why can't we go on a mini-break? Why? Why? Why?' 'That's a good idea,' said Daniel mildly. 'Why don't you book somewhere for next weekend? Nice country house hotel. I'll pay.' "
From *Bridget Jones's Diary* by
HELEN FIELDING

Defining idea . . .

141

- Burn some incense. Ylang ylang, rose, and sandalwood are sensual scents and help create a sexy atmosphere.
- Think soft lighting. A room lit by a fluorescent strip light or, worse still, a turned-down television, will never be a boudoir. A row of tea lights down a windowsill or in front of a mirror, on the other hand, is very effective.

How did it go?

Q   I'd like to whisk my girlfriend away for a wild weekend, but I can't afford even the cheapest bed-and-breakfast. Is there an alternative?

A   *Don't despair. We've had hard times, too, but still had fantastic breaks without re-mortgaging our home. We've used several ruses, including going away midweek when many hotels and guesthouses do special offers, collecting special-offer coupons from newspapers for cheap foreign travel, last-minute Internet sites, and befriending people with large country homes. Remember when your parents said love is about making sacrifices? They were right. We're going to be bold and suggest you give up something like smoking or café lattes for a month and splurge your savings on your partner.*

Q   I took my husband on a short golfing vacation, but we spent the whole time arguing. Why didn't it work for us?

A   *This sounds like catch-up fighting. When couples have spent time apart or have been so busy with work or domestic stuff that there hasn't been time to talk and sort out little problems, resentments get stored up. The first chance you have to be together, you catch up on all sorts of things, especially grievances. Try it again, now that you've gotten it out of your system.*

33

Bedroom eyes

Want a really racy relationship? You need a bedroom to match. We'll help you create a retreat from the rest of the world, a haven from household hassles, an oasis from office stress.

It's hard to pursue private passions if you're tiptoeing around the laundry basket or in danger of upsetting a Reader's Digest mountain. Make over your bedroom, then make out in style.

What does your bedroom say about your relationship? Is it warm and inviting? Dramatic, with no-holds-barred color? Fresh, clean, and confident? Or cluttered, messy, and stuck in another era of your lives?

Turn your bedroom into a boudoir. For a bedroom that's vibrant and exhilarating, commanding yet calm, the trick is to think sassy, not trashy. Think wrought-iron four-poster bed, plump throw pillows, and antique candelabras rather than black sheets, red lightbulbs, and mirrors on the ceiling. And not a hint of chintz.

Exploit the position of your bedroom. For instance, if it's south facing, avoid heavy curtains and opt for lighter billowy drapes to enjoy opaque morning light seeping

143

Here's an idea for you . . .

If you're not able to do a major makeover just yet, keeping your bedroom tidy and clutter-free is a good start. Once you've exiled the junk, put a vase of fresh flowers on the bedside table, display a couple of photos of the two of you, and treat yourself to some new bed linens.

into your lives as you wake. If you've only got a small room, cultivate a cozy, intimate feel with intense colors and quirky lamps.

If you yearn for a room that's decadent and enticing, go for an ornate style, with voluptuous velvets. Whatever style you choose, crisp cotton bedsheets are essential. Some people like the thought of silk, but you'll find your partner slipping away from you. For sensual bliss, think textures and layers. Could you put velvet, silk, or fur throws over those crisp cotton sheets?

Pastel colors teamed with silver and white accessories create a dreamy and tranquil haven. You might like to hang some vintage wallpaper, or a modern imitation. Either way, pick out one or two key colors and use them in your soft furnishings. Jazz up thrift shop finds with distressed paint techniques, or show off a sexy dress on a tailor's dummy. Antique hatboxes or designer luggage are glamorous storage solutions. A chest of draper's drawers makes a stunning showcase for lingerie and linens.

If you think boudoirs are all about Barbie dolls, forget it. Your bedroom doesn't have to be toe-curlingly frilly or feminine; boudoirs can be butch. How about painting the walls with manly denim and silver stripes, or deep Moroccan blues to match mosaic-topped bedside tables, accessorized with Moorish mirrors? Or for something more fiery, why not take inspiration from the Arabian Nights? Spice-colored saris, which you can buy in a specialist sari shop or online, come in a fantastic range of colors and lush fabrics. Use them as throws over the bed. Draw inspiration from the jewel colors of the Far East and paint one wall in deep red, scarlet, or fuchsia. If you paint the other walls a lighter shade, it will stop them from closing in on you. Or go gothic, with black-framed pictures and mirrors, and tall, ornate candlesticks. But no gargoyles or you'll end up with a bedroom that's more Addams Family than period allure.

Stuck for inspiration? Why not steal ideas from boutique hotels? Research boudoir chic one weekend. See IDEA 32, April in Paris.

Try another idea...

MAKES SCENTS

Use smell to carry the theme through. Scented candles, oil burners, or incense can all be utilized to float soothing scents around your boudoir. Next time you wash your bedsheets, add a few drops of lavender oil to the rinse cycle.

ANIMAL MAGIC

If you're a wild tiger or glamour puss at heart, scatter some fake animal fur–print cushions or invest in a faux leopard rug. Don't take it too far though. The leopard-print thongs are best left in the joke shop.

SOUNDS GOOD

If you don't have music piped into your bedroom, keep a basic CD player close to the bed, with a few favorite albums at hand. It doesn't need to be all singing and dancing, but a continuous-play button comes in handy.

"It doesn't matter what you do in the bedroom as long as you don't do it in the street and frighten the horses."
MRS. PATRICK CAMPBELL, actress

Defining idea...

LIGHT UP YOUR LIFE

You already know a neon strip light is a bad idea and probably already have pink-toned lightbulbs in your bedroom. But for a magical night, nothing compares to the glow from a candlelit chandelier.

How did it go?

Q   We live in a rented accommodation and our landlord won't let us redecorate. The walls are plain white and our bedroom looks drab. We don't really need to sex up our bedroom as we've got each other, but if we did, how would you suggest we go about it?

A   *You can still create a stunning room by working with what you've got. Experiment with different colored bedsheets, perhaps according to seasons. Accessorize with matching candles and scents. So you could have pastel green sheets in spring, with apple incense and vases of exotic grasses, or hot pink sheets in winter with berry-colored candles and vanilla scents.*

Q   We live in a loft and are minimalists. How can we prevent our sleeping area from being too austere and make it more inviting without drastically changing our lifestyle?

A   *Go monochrome. Cream is softer than plain white. Cream sheets, a couple of strategically placed tall pillar candles, and a large vase of lilies will help you create understated elegance. To create a sense of privacy without losing space, invest in a simple screen.*

146

34

You look wonderful tonight

When you first met, you felt a little flutter every time you saw each other. Give your old flame first-date butterflies with a makeover that brings out the best in both of you.

Just because he's seen your bikini line in "relaxed" mode doesn't mean you can't still turn his head. All you need is a little application...

KEEP IT PERSONAL

Looking wonderful on short notice doesn't have to mean panic-buying clothes and products that end up at the back of the wardrobe or bathroom cabinet sooner rather than later. Many department stores offer a free personal shopper service for men and women. An hour's consultation is worth several trips rushing around the stores solo, and it's more likely to get you results. Be up front. Explain that you want a look to make your long-term lover weak at the knees rather than weak in the stomach. The shopper should then bring you a selection of styles to suit your size, frame, personality, and budget. The best ones won't force new trends on you, but adapt fashions to suit your style. It's up to you whether you love it or leave it.

Here's an idea for you . . . Wouldn't it be great if you could take the afternoon off and spend it at a spa before meeting your partner in the evening? Most of us can't do this very often, but you can achieve a similar effect in about twenty minutes. Guys, pop into an old-fashioned barbershop for a really close shave. Women, befriend a department store makeup counter assistant. Say something like, "I'm happy with my look for work, but I want to look sexier in the evenings." You'll get a free makeover, using all the latest tricks and techniques. "Test" some new perfume as you go out and you're set to wow him.

Defining idea . . .

"You have to remember that before two hours of hair and makeup even I don't look like Cindy Crawford."
CINDY CRAWFORD, supermodel

CUTTING EDGE

There's no quicker way to change your partner's reaction from ho-hum to wow than by blowing your budget at the hairdresser. A short back and sides, gamine crop, or simply highlighting your tresses before having them professionally styled can transform you in your lunch hour. While we're talking about hair, be a smooth operator and get rid of any facial hair (nose and ears, too).

HONEY I SHRUNK THE COSMETICS BILL

They say beauty is skin deep. But what do you do if you've run out of cleanser, toner, or moisturizer, and you're going out in twenty minutes? Raid the cupboard. Honey will give you a gorgeous glow. It's a great cleanser and moisturizer combo, and smells delicious. Massage a little into your wet face and as you rub it off, it exfoliates all those dulling dead cells into the bargain. If you've got a little longer, mix a teaspoon of honey with a tablespoon of yogurt and use it as a face mask. Or spread it on other rough, dry places, like feet or elbows. Leave for ten minutes and rinse. Take some in the shower with you, too, as it's a great conditioner that leaves your hair smelling delicious.

Sex has been shown to slow signs of aging. Need any more excuses? Check out IDEA 38, Sex.

Try another idea . . .

THE EYES HAVE IT

Get that come-hither look by plucking your eyebrows into shape. Yes, even men— eyebrows that meet in the middle make you look like Dracula, and you know what trouble he had keeping a woman! If you haven't got time to do full eye makeup, a whip of mascara can transform your look, drawing attention to your eyes. Many metrosexual men already know mascara also comes in clear.

HAND IT TO YOU

Eyes may be the windows of the soul, but when you reach out to touch your partner, how often is it with silky smooth hands rather than ones chapped and worn by washing dishes, gardening, or typing? A calloused caress isn't very sexy. If you usually work *with* your hands, it's time to get to work *on* your hands. Smooth rough hands by mixing some sea salt with some olive oil and rubbing it all over them. A few strokes with a nail buffer means you can leave nails in the buff if you haven't time to polish up your act with color.

"As Ursula is my girlfriend of many years, I naturally rarely look at her anymore. I register that her outline is there, rather than actually looking at her. Purely for your benefit, however, I'll go rummaging around in the untidy basement of my memory to see if I can find where I left her features."
MIL MILLINGTON, newspaper columnist and author of *Things My Girlfriend and I Have Argued About*

Defining idea . . .

149

How did
it go?

Q **My husband and I get along pretty well, but it upsets me that he doesn't seem to appreciate the time and trouble I take to look good for him. I still have my figure, but he doesn't notice when I've had my hair done or bought a new dress. Is there anything I can do to knock him off his feet?**

A *Sadly, some husbands just don't notice how their wives look and have little interest in their own appearance. It could be a sign of indifference, or perhaps he's more interested in your inner beauty. Dress for yourself and enjoy the positive attention you get elsewhere.*

Q **I'm not sure how to put this. I wish my girlfriend would make more of herself. She's a lovely person with little personal vanity, but she is up for new ideas. I'd like to get her a new outfit but don't know where to start. Any suggestions?**

A *Lots of women's magazines use real people as models for before-and-after makeover features. The results can be dramatic. Nominate your girlfriend and give her a day she'll never forget. She'll learn lots of useful hints to help her make the most of her strong points and conceal the rest.*

35

With a little help from your friends

Your friends can change your relationship for the better, but you might have to change them for better friends. Time to clear out your address book as you would old clothes.

Discussing old friends in the same sentences as tank tops, miniskirts, or go-go boots might seem heartless, but this book is about facing hard facts and finding new solutions.

If you can recognize friends and other couples who can help you re-energize, you'll get a revamped social life as well as a richer relationship. Sadly, some friends have a stake in keeping your relationship how it is. Call us callous, but they have to be jilted before you can enjoy the love life you really want.

Everyone changes: individuals as well as couples. Friends from school, colleagues from the workplace, people from the neighborhood. Maybe you've been lucky enough to find friends early who stay with you for life, able to adapt to changing

Here's an idea for you . . .

Conduct an address book audit. Take a deep breath, go through your address book, and ask some serious questions: Do we feel happy and comfortable as a couple with these people? What role do I play when I'm with this person? Is that role good for my relationship? Which friendships undermine our commitment? While you're at it, why not see if there's anyone you could get to know better? Ask them out for a double date with their partner and take it from there. It might not work, but you'll never know until you give it your best shot.

circumstances and needs, and get on with your partner effortlessly. In an ideal world, friends provide unlimited support, excitement, compassion, and enjoyment, from cradle to crematorium. In truth, most don't last the course, rather staying for one particular episode and slowly fading away. Maybe you are drawn together at work by a shared hatred of a particular manager yet outside work you have little in common. Foursome friendships, where you and your partner hang out with another couple, can be like that: great when you all have kids of similar ages, but once you've exchanged news of Johnny and Jessica there's an uncomfortable silence.

Friends who want to keep your relationship just as it is are not conniving or manipulative (well, some might be). Many friendships depend on us playing set roles: mother, office superstar, or immoral wild child. When your relationship changes, these roles change, too. When Daniel started spending more time with Petula rather than at the tennis club, his drinking buddies started to nag and tease him. His friends didn't set out to undermine his efforts to reconnect with his partner, but because he'd become a bit of a stranger, they tried to cajole him back into a familiar role.

There are also some people who seem magnetically drawn to problems and misery. If you're going through a bad patch in your relationship, they'll be there to lend an ear, but you'll have to pay them back with interest. If you're getting along fine with your partner,

Salsa classes, tea dances, and line dancing are great places to cultivate new friendships. See IDEA 26, *Let's face the music and dance.*

Try another idea . . .

they won't want to hear about your romantic weekend together but will probe you for your next potential problem. One thing we've been surprised by is just how few friends want to share our good times and triumphs. It's not malice, just life. If their relationship falls short, seeing yours improve can be threatening or a cause for jealousy.

Instead, fill your lives with people you admire, who inspire you and who will support you. Your new friends should have some of the following qualities (if they have them all, move in immediately):

■ Couples where you like and get on with both partners equally.
■ Couples in relationships where no one is the boss.
■ Couples who are great listeners, who seem interested in you and your lives.
■ Positive people who are prepared to try new things.
■ People who share your sense of humor and fun.
■ Couples prepared to give your joint relationship as much time and effort as you.
■ People who are great mixers, who get on with your family and other friends, and who you are happy to see in any company.
■ People you can talk to when you or they are unhappy about something.
■ People who reciprocate hospitality.
■ People who don't take sides in one of your arguments.

FRIENDS TO AVOID

We know that you already give a wide berth to couples where one or both are bores, hypochondriacs, or egocentrics. But like us, you've probably discovered that some friends and couples who seemed okay turn out to be friends from hell, intent on stirring up trouble and resentment between you and your partner. Banish these types:

- Snipers: people who drop envious comments about your house, job, car, relationship, or lifestyle.
- Control freaks: some couples and individuals have to dominate. This is bad news whether it is conversation subject matter or where you'll eat. These sorts of choices ought to be mutual.
- Bloodsuckers: friends who are affected with contagious forms of negativity. Spend an evening in their company and you need a week to recover.
- Sulkers: "friends" unable to accept that you can't always drop everything and have a meal with them at two hours' notice. They'll make you feel guilty.

 Defining idea...

"God gave us our relatives; thank God we can choose our friends."
ETHEL WATTS MUMFORD, writer

Q   Help. My wife and I have dined at our friends' home a number of   *How did*
times. I think they are getting resentful because we never invite   *it go?*
them back. We don't because my wife doesn't think our cooking is
up to their standard. I don't think it matters, but she won't budge
and it's causing scenes. How do we get around this problem?

A   *Take them out for Indian food and pay the bill before the coffee arrives.*

Q   My partner doesn't like a lot of my female friends; he thinks
they're shallow and image conscious. I always have fun and come
home buzzing after a night out with them. Do I have to give them
up?

A   *No way! It's important that you keep and cultivate them. Your partner*
doesn't want to drink cocktails and compare new lipsticks, but that's no big
deal. Having separate friends and social lives is an important way of
maintaining your independence, which is essential for a healthy relationship.
If you gave them the boot, it wouldn't be long before you felt like showing
him the door, too.

36

Love and marriage

Do they really go together like a horse and carriage? We don't know, but we do know that arranging and tailoring your own special day gives your relationship a boost that lasts.

A marriage certificate may just be a piece of paper, but the emotional investments, legal ties, and public declarations made in front of your mom and best friends make it your most important possession.

Living in sin? Marriage has a lot going for it, you know. Cohabiting comes with legal implications, like not being recognized as your partner's next of kin. And let's face it: people never take your relationship that seriously if you're only living together. Yes it's sexist, but we've noticed it's usually guys who are reluctant to tie the knot. Maybe you're a commitment-phobe? Already notched up one or more unsuccessful marriages? Enjoying the disapproval of parents or landlords? Get over it.

Here's an idea for you . . . **Been married for years? Dust off the album, reminisce over the good times, and then renew your vows. Like your wedding dress, some might not fit anymore. Perhaps you'll want to make some new ones, or use your own rather than the prescribed wording.**

WHAT A DIFFERENCE "I DO" MAKES

Publicly promising to stay with your partner forever profoundly changes your relationship. Making or renewing vows buttresses previous promises. Marriage is a chance to stop and think about what we want for our relationships and what we need to get there. Like it or not, his 'n' hers gleaming gold bands affect how others treat your relationship. When you merely live together, it can be more easily undermined. Once the landlord or office bitch has heard about your nuptials or witnessed you making legally binding ties, it's hard to keep treating you like a live-in floozy.

WEDDING BLISS

Heard that weddings are stressful and strain relationships? Not if you ignore the propaganda peddled by the wedding industry. Rushing around trying to find the last four hundred of this season's must-have sugared almond holders in pale yellow will frazzle your nerves and your partner's patience. Instead, work together to create a day as personal and individual as your relationship. We had a lot of fun designing our own invitations and took massive pleasure thinking of the money we saved. Want to go one further? Try to find a place where you can design and make your own wedding rings. You know your partner better than us, and if you're worried you'll have to wear something that looks as if it's come from junior craft class, get a store-bought ring and have it inscribed with a secret or personal message—something that will give you a secret thrill whenever you read it. Laws governing the wedding ceremony vary from country to country, but in most places you can personalize your vows, add your own rituals to more traditional ones, or go the whole hog and do it yourself. Perhaps you'd love to get married underwater, in a hot-air balloon, or even via e-mail. In most countries you can, but you may need a civil ceremony as well to cover all the legal bits.

Pop the question over a candlelit dinner at home. See IDEA 39, *You are what you eat.*

Try another idea . . .

The more you involve family and friends in the preparation, the more supported you'll feel during the day and beyond. Our family helped us make the invitations, and we wrote a ceremony that included favorite readings and poems, live jazz, and solo vocalists. Swedish songs, a Pakistani wedding dance, and disco club classics were also part of our celebration. If your reception reflects the uniqueness of your union as well as your commitment, you can't lose.

"Marriage is a bribe to make a housekeeper think she's a householder."
From *The Merchant of Yonkers* by THORNTON WILDER

Defining idea . . .

STRAIGHT TALKING

If you think weddings are sexist, homophobic nonsense, all about archaic property transfer rights and keeping money in the family, you're absolutely right! But not all weddings are, and certainly not the sort we have in mind. There's no reason why you and your same-sex partner can't cherry-pick the best bits to create an unforgettable commitment ceremony. Commitment doesn't have to be legal to be powerful or life changing. Nevertheless, some couples do include legally binding arrangements, like wills or property ownership.

"Marriage is popular because it combines the maximum of temptation with the maximum of opportunity."
GEORGE BERNARD SHAW

Defining idea . . .

159

How did it go?

Q **My fiancé and I would love to arrange a personalized wedding but I know it would cause terrible trouble with my parents. I'm their only daughter and my mom has been dreaming about a big white church wedding since I was little. How can I not disappoint her and my dad but still have what I want?**

A *You could, of course, put your foot down and do your own thing. Then again, the views of the people who brought you up and cared for you are important, and weddings are special family occasions. Why don't you and your fiancé sit down and talk to both sets of parents and see if there's any middle ground? If that doesn't get you anywhere, you could go with your mom's white wedding and have a more personal gathering for friends on another occasion. Two parties for the price of one.*

Q **We've tried to write our own vows, but everything we write sounds tacky or flowery. Can you suggest anything?**

A *The word "vow" seems to bring on the frilliest, silliest language. Why not make a list of expectations you each have for your relationship, and see if you can convert these into a list of promises? If you want to add color, keep your own words simple but include a paragraph from a favorite book or film, or ask your best man to read a poem.*

37

What a difference a day makes

Tightening belts may be good for the soul, but it's lousy for the spirit. Do something amazing today. Surprise your partner, go all out and spoil her rotten. You know she's worth it.

Living within our means is a good goal, but day after day it's really boring. The occasional splurge may seem expensive, but it can re-energize you and your partner.

Sometimes your relationship needs a life-changing day. Perhaps you're both sick of the same routine? Husband having a hard time at work? Need to make your twenty-fifth Valentine's Day as dynamic as the first? Just moved? Or the best reason of all: Just because.

We suggest starting your amazing day the night before. Spring a surprise on your partner: prebook the best suite in a nearby hotel. Waking up in a mahogany four-poster bed will make the most jaded couple feel like royalty. It's the perfect start to a wonderful day, one without the hassle of work, chores, telephones, or e-mail. Use this

Here's an idea for you . . .

This evening, turn your dining area into a five-star restaurant. Prepare a handwritten menu of your partner's favorite dishes, put her kind of music on in the background, and cook as much as possible beforehand so you're not tied to the kitchen. Do something special in between courses. Play the piano, read her a poem, look into her eyes and tell her what you see.

day to do something totally different. Treat your partner like an off-duty Hollywood superstar and arrange a series of treats that goes something like this:

GOOD MORNING TO YOU, MA'AM

After hotel breakfast in bed, arrange to be collected by a chauffeur-driven limousine and taken to a special event. You might go to the station to pick up a luxury train, or visit a racetrack or yachting regatta. Alternatively you could use a vintage Rolls-Royce or, if the distance isn't too great, a horse and carriage or bicycle rickshaw. If a sporting event or railway journey isn't your partner's thing, why not arrange a private guided tour of a favorite gallery or museum, followed by lunch?

VERY GOOD AFTERNOON TO YOU, SIR

Lunch is a cinch, but indulging in a proper champagne tea is an all-but-forgotten pleasure. As the name suggests, you start with a glass of vintage champagne. Toast each other, the both of you, or the sheer decadence; the idea is to enjoy! It doesn't matter if he then chooses exotic orange blossom or refreshing peppermint tea; just insist that the crusts are cut off his sandwiches, which should be followed by fruit scones or pastries, a large wedge of sumptuous chocolate cake, or a tangy lemon tart. Let your meal go down over a little light window-shopping; stroll in an exclusive neighborhood or browse antique stores—whatever makes your partner tick.

HAPPY HOUR

Time for happy hour in a trendy cocktail bar. Get into the groove by dressing as if for the Oscars and make sure your chauffeur opens all the doors for your love, for tonight he's the winner. Today is about being classy not crass, so avoid unsubtly named lurid concoctions like Sex on the Beach, or A Long Hard Screw, and instead order a large classy Cosmopolitan or Bellini, with two straws.

THAT'S SHOWBIZ

Now on to a show. If she likes the movies, go to the biggest, plushest theater in town. Bring a blanket for her knees and snuggle. If you go to the theater or opera, book a box and order champagne for the intermission.

FINISHING TOUCHES

Give your evening meal the movie-star treatment. Write a love letter or card and ask the waiter to hide it in your partner's menu. Have your loved one serenaded by a singer or musician; present him with an item of jewelry between the main course and dessert. It doesn't have to be a ring; it could be a watch or chain. And why not have flowers delivered to the restaurant after coffee? After you've eaten, don't just go to the beach; go for a barefoot sunset stroll along the sand and surprise him with that calf-leather wallet he's been drooling over.

Think you can't afford a day like this? Clear out your clutter and hold a sale. Your old trash could become someone's treasure. Check out IDEA 27, *Dump your junk.*

Try another idea...

"*Love is like any other luxury. You have no right to it unless you can afford it.*"
From *The Way We Live Now* by ANTHONY TROLLOPE

Defining idea...

"*Give us the luxuries of life, and we will dispense with its necessities.*"
JOHN LOTHROP MOTLEY, nineteenth-century diplomat

Defining idea...

163

How did it go?

Q   My wife has traveled to England a number of times and loves it. I'd love to do something special that would be the highlight of our next trip. Any suggestions?

A   What about a trip in a hot-air balloon? You can take one from almost anywhere and, depending on the wind direction, you'll have an opportunity to get a great view of the countryside or a city. They tend to fly during the summer months—either early in the morning, which means getting up before sunrise, or in the evening. Looking down on what appears to be a huge model train set with moving cars and ant-sized people is a never-to-be-forgotten treat. Most journeys last around an hour, and after landing you will be collected and normally offered a glass of champagne.

Q   We had a wonderful day at the races and it's one I will never forget. I put everything on my credit card and got an awful shock when the bill arrived. How can I get myself back in the black?

A   These things happen. We guess that you'll have to forgo a luxury or two for a while, or maybe do a little overtime. But, over time, when you have wiped out your overdraft, we hope that you'll be able to look back on the day with pleasure and save and budget for future treats.

38

Sex

Has your sex life dwindled from three times a day to three times a year? Giving it up completely for a while might be the best way to rev it up.

Lost interest in sex? Bored in the bedroom? Perhaps your partner's turn-ons, once so electrifying, now turn you off. Maybe you're coming too soon or not at all?

If your sex life has hit the doldrums, don't despair, you're not alone. A large Dutch study found that 26 percent of men and 43 percent of women had problems with sexual enjoyment or arousal. Twelve percent of men and 33 percent of women weren't having satisfactory orgasms; 5 percent of women weren't having orgasms at all. The good news? You can sort these problems out together, following a plan that starts with you giving up sex.

STOP HAVING SEX AND PUT THE ZING BACK INTO YOUR SEX LIFE

Doesn't sound right, does it? But in the sixties and seventies, sexperts William Masters and Virginia Johnson discovered a formula for building up sexual tension that will make you both explode with lust. It's called sensate focus, and it involves spending time at different stages, only moving on to the next when you both feel happy and comfortable with the stage you're at. Here's what you do:

Here's an idea for you . . .

Too tired for sex after a night on the dance floor? Try thinking of sex as a starter instead of a dessert. Once you're dressed to party, invite your partner to a private party of your own. Don't be a prude; hitch your skirt up in the hallway and enjoy a quick romp. The best part? Exchanging those knowing "cat that got the cream" looks all night.

Stage 1

Set aside time to take turns to touch each other. Take turns being the "toucher," finding ways of touching your partner for your own pleasure. You can touch anywhere except your partner's genitals or breasts.

Stage 2

In this stage, if you are the "toucher" you can touch your partner anywhere except the genitals or breasts for both your pleasure and your partner's.

Stage 3

Now you can touch your partner anywhere, including the genitals and breasts, but sexual intercourse is still off-limits.

Stage 4

Time to touch your partner while your partner touches you anywhere, including your genitals, but don't have sexual intercourse. We know, you're getting desperate—but it'll be worth the wait.

Defining idea . . .

Stage 5

When your partner feels ready, you can put your penis inside her. Relax and breathe together. But no thrusting. Gradually increase the length of time you keep your penis inside her.

"You mustn't force sex to do the work of love, or love the work of sex."
MARY MCCARTHY, writer

Stage 6
Anything goes now, so go for it.

Some sex therapists suggest couples book lovemaking times into their planners, just as you schedule time for board meetings. Although this stops busy couples from overlooking sex, it doesn't work for everyone. If you thrive on spontaneity, seize the moment. Avoid putting off sex because you haven't got time for a three-hour love-in. A quickie is better than nothing, and the more sex you have, the more you'll feel like having.

It's not very easy to get down and get dirty if you have to move a laptop, three weeks worth of laundry, and a pile of fly-fishing magazines out of the way first. Find out how to create your own love temple by turning your bedroom into a boudoir in IDEA 33, *Bedroom eyes.*

Try another idea . . .

TALKING DIRTY

Your partner doesn't know what you want until you tell him. If you find it difficult to launch into a spontaneous discussion about how you've always wanted to have sex on the porch under the spider plant with the lights on, have a round of truth or dare. Alternatively, start a raunchy requests box. Whenever you hear or think of something new you'd like to try, write it down and put it into your box. It could be a position (draw stickmen), location, fantasy, or role-play. Once a month, both of you pick an idea from the other's box, but don't show the other what you've picked. Before the end of the month, surprise your lover with his heart's desire.

"Remember, if you smoke after sex you're doing it too fast."
WOODY ALLEN

Defining idea . . .

Q **Our love life has never been very good because whatever I try seems to hurt my wife. We've tried sensate focus, but can't get beyond stage five because my wife says it's still painful. What can we do?**

A *There may be a physical or psychological cause for her pain. Inadequate lubrication is the most common reason, and can be helped with a water-based lubricant. We suggest she visits her doctor, though, as infections or allergic reactions to spermicide or latex can also cause pain. Vaginismus, where the vagina contracts, making intercourse painful or impossible, is often secondary to sexual abuse, rape, and injuries to the vagina. It is possible to overcome it with specialist sex therapy. Don't worry, nobody will make you have sex in front of them. You'll be given homework exercises and asked to report back. Improve your relationship by being sensitive to your wife, and seek medical support.*

Q **I have a greater sex drive than my partner. We never made love a lot, but the frequency has dwindled to less than once a month in recent years. I've tried everything: sexy underwear, stunning nighties, candlelight in the bedroom. Most often he gives me a nice kiss then turns over and falls asleep. Is there any hope?**

A *We all have different libidos, but this will only cause frustration if yours is vastly different from your partner's—which yours is. If the root cause is your partner's unfitness, you could try exercising together; the extra testosterone generated could be enough to tilt the balance. If you are feeling rejected by him, you could encourage him to become more demonstrative physically and treat this as an end in itself.*

39

You are what you eat

Eating the same old boring food is a recipe for ruining a relationship. Egg your partner on to refresh your plates and refresh your palates for each other.

When relationships are new, we're happy cooking special suppers or having breakfast in bed. But familiarity breeds cereal bars on the bus, TV dinners, bar food, and favorite family restaurants.

BREAKFAST

Young lovers excepted, the only people who are served breakfast in bed are hospital patients. A pity, as being served by your loved one is a great way to start any day. A hearty breakfast with all the trimmings gives both of you a real incentive to work off all those thousands of calories. If you can't face bacon, sausages, and French toast, there are lighter alternatives. Why strawberries taste better in bed is a mystery but it's true, especially if you are fed by the apple of your eye.

Stuck in a rut? Do something different. Shop somewhere else this week. How about that Chinese supermarket? If there's no grocery store off the beaten path, go to your local supermarket, but buy ten things you've never eaten before.

FOOD FOR LOVE

Spaghetti again? Staying with safe staples can make your romantic liaison feel past its sell-by date. Instead, serve up some oysters. Apart from their obvious similarities with women's bits, they're rich in zinc—a trace element essential for healthy sex organs. You probably know oysters are only in season when there's an "r" in the month, but caviar or mussels do the trick, too. Or how about a few asparagus spears tossed in butter? Very phallic in shape, if not in size or color. They can be eaten suggestively as foreplay to a main course or intercourse.

When it comes to presentation, look at cookbook photos for inspiration. Pile food in the middle of a plate and drizzle dressings and sauces around it. Think about how you eat, too. Scarfing down your food or slurping your soup are two top turn-offs. If this sounds unpleasantly familiar, why not eat in front of a mirror next time you're on your own and practice looking seductive? And don't forget to take a napkin.

SPICE UP YOUR LIFE

Fresh herbs and spices add zing to any meal. Instead of walking in with wilted gas station tulips, bring home some herbs. The great thing about herbs is that they grow anywhere. You don't need a special herb garden; a couple of pots on a windowsill will do the job. Bash out your frustrations with a pestle and mortar instead of taking work stresses out on your beloved. Like it hot? Red chili peppers are a proven aphrodisiac.

JUST DESSERTS

Let's face it; if you've cooked a main meal from scratch, nobody will be disappointed if you cheat with a store-bought dessert. A few squares of dark chocolate is all you need. Chocolate contains phenyethylamine, which is the same chemical our brains produce when we fall in love. Candles and sparklers add pizzazz to any brownies fresh out of the box. Stuart put small squares on saucers, stuck a small sparkler in each, and turned off the main light before carrying them to the table. The effect was magical; suffice it to say that the next course wasn't coffee.

Grow your own aphrodisiacs. See IDEA 49, *Sowing the seeds of love.*

Try another idea . . .

"Sex without champagne is like taking a bus instead of a chauffeur-driven limousine— you'll get there in the end but not in anything like the same style. Sex with wine is marginally better, but whether you're traveling in a Jaguar or a Ford Escort will depend on the quality of the wine. There is no doubt that alcohol is a social lubricant and, with its ability to relax and lower inhibitions, it can be a lover's little helper."
From *Aphrodisiac* by MARION MCGILVARY

Defining idea . . .

171

Defining idea...

"The only thing better than breakfast in bed is lunch in bed."
JOHN O'FARRELL, journalist and novelist

ALCOHOL

You hardly need us to tell you that booze is a mixed blessing. A couple of glasses of half-decent red or white can make even a modest meal special, yet a couple more can make you slurred and silly. Small amounts of alcohol can make you feel sexy and modest amounts can make you a bit loose, but larger amounts just make you sleepy.

INVEST IN A JUICER AND ICE CREAM MAKER

Juicers get the juices going. Homemade rhubarb ice cream or a freshly made fruit smoothie is the sort of heavenly treat grown men would walk across water for just to get a second helping. Juicers and ice cream makers are easy to use and great fun, and once you've tasted the fruits of your own work, you won't want to go back to the supermarket variety again.

Q **I always have to do the cooking by myself, and to rub salt into the wound I have to wash up as well. Is there hope or will I always be tied to the kitchen sink?**

How did it go?

A *Well, Cinderella, in the absence of a fairy godmother, we suggest you buy her a recipe book for her next birthday. The new glossy ones are worth getting for the mouthwatering photos alone. And get a pair of rubber gloves—they'll at least keep your wound dry.*

Q **We find time to cook together on weekends, but during the week we end up relying on the same old ready-made meals and takeout. We prefer our own food, but how can we find the time?**

A *If you have a few kitchen gadgets, cooking for four or six takes hardly any longer than cooking for two. Why not cook double or triple portions and freeze what you don't eat during the weekend for use during the week? Heating up frozen food in a microwave takes about as long as phoning for takeout, and you won't have to wait an hour for it to be delivered.*

40

How deep is the ocean?

Revitalize your relationship by dressing up in smooth, skintight wet suits and strapping on some fancy equipment. Get set to explore some warm, wet places. Come on down.

Exploring wrecked ships could be a lifeline for shipwrecked relationships. Whether you wade in the shallows or snorked in the sea, scuba diving can take your relationship to a new level.

SCUBA SCHOOL

Scuba diving combines a thrilling adrenaline rush with the soothing properties of water and the enthusiasm that comes from shared learning. There are few thrills that can equal your first dive. If you've been there and done it already, taking your partner is almost as good again. Practically any healthy couple with reasonable fitness will be able to complete the knowledge tests and pool and open-water dives necessary to gain a basic diving qualification, allowing you to dive together anywhere in the world.

Visit a diving school. Many offer free trial dives in a pool. A pro will get you fitted out and give you both a chance to see if you're up for going further.

COUPLES WHO DIVE TOGETHER, THRIVE TOGETHER

Our relationship is always revived when we check in to Sharm el Sheikh, by the Red Sea. We love to float about in what feels like a marine tank while discovering zillions of fish in beautiful colors and masses of coral. It's as if we've been to paradise. There was a time when diving was a guy thing. Those days are long past. Training at home or on vacation is very affordable, and more and more couples are taking the plunge. Over one million people learn to scuba dive every year. Many of them have found out that diving is a first-rate activity for couples seeking a deeper connection. And as it's noncompetitive, it makes an ideal couple sport.

"Although her tank still had plenty of air, Rose came up with me and those few minutes making that safety stop were the best diving that I had ever had. We hung there together in the shallow waters where the light was dazzling, the coral reef shining like a treasure chest, watching a school of angel fish swarm around us as our bubbles of air mixed together and rose lazily to the surface."
TONY PARSONS, journalist and novelist

BUDDY UP

Divers always dive with a "buddy." In your case, buddy up with your partner. It sounds obvious, we know, but make sure your course leader knows you're together before you're paired up with someone else. Buddies stick together underwater. Together, you'll build up a fund of joint experiences from your escapades. You'll have to look out for each other, too. You'll develop deeper trust for each other as, theoretically, you might both have to breathe out of the same regulator. You'll learn this so-called "buddy breathing" in scuba courses. It's exhilarating. If your buddy is in trouble, it's up to you to alert someone. You'll learn survival skills like the tired diver tow, where you drag a tired partner to shore (usually the side of the pool). Because you'll both have a responsibility for each other and potentially be in a position to save your partner's life, diving builds immense trust and lasting confidence in each other.

You'll also have to learn ways to communicate nonverbally underwater. There are universally understood gestures you'll be taught for letting your buddy know, for example, that you want to go up or down, or that something is wrong. Learning to communicate without words has important residual effects for communication on dry land, too. When it comes to intimate relationships, nonverbal communication is actually more important than verbal communication. And as the saying goes, "Underwater, no one can hear you nag."

Try another idea...

Like the sound of an adrenaline surge but don't want to get your hair wet? Check out IDEA 28, *Hike up the heartbeat.*

...and another

Found your waterwings? For other ways of using water to refresh your relationship, have a look at IDEA 42, *Making a splash.*

Defining idea...

"*Diving's great for relationships because you can't argue underwater.*"
DR. SARA SCHROTER, senior researcher for *British Medical Journal* and diving enthusiast

Defining idea...

"*He who would search for pearls must dive below.*"
JOHN DRYDEN, poet, dramatist, and literary critic

How did it go?

Q **We're taking a diving course together. I love it, but my boyfriend keeps panicking and pulling off his gear. I tell him it's just like being in a womb, but he says, "Why do you think I got born?" What else can I try?**

A *Sounds like you're a natural mermaid. But most people panic when they first try to breathe underwater. Have some fun with him by practicing breathing using a regulator in the bath. Blowing bubbles from both ends of his body should amuse him. If you help him catch up between classes, you'll get top marks in your relationship.*

Q **We've done a trial dive in our local pool. It was fun, but nothing amazing. How can we find out if this will really improve our relationship, before spending a lot more money?**

A *All right, we admit it. Seeing the bottom of our local pool and a few pebbles up close doesn't do much for us either. If you're not sure about shelling out for the course, we suggest you plan your next trip away close to a dive center. Many offer a trial dive in the sea, where you'll be taken down by a dive master. It's a great chance to make your mind up as well as experiencing firsthand some of the sights we're raving about.*

41

Snap, cackle, and print

Want a picture-perfect relationship? Whether you're groping around in your home darkroom or shooting your partner outdoors, photography can put your relationship back into sharp focus. Give it your best shot.

Camera shy or just shy with cameras? We'll show you how to feel comfortable on either side of the lens. Couples who shoot together stay together, as they share a developing interest.

LIFE THROUGH A LENS

We live in a visual age, where pictures or images rather than words are the major means of telling stories. Most of us own a camera. Sadly, most cameras are used thoughtlessly (if at all), hastily pointed at family reunions, resulting in drab snaps. But your humble camera can help you develop a vivid, vibrant relationship. Photography helps you see and interpret circumstances differently. It enhances communication as you develop new ways of enlightening, informing, amusing, and persuading each other. Pack a couple of disposable cameras the next time you go out. As you document special moments or record unforgettable experiences, you'll make images that are personal and special to the love of your life.

Here's an
idea for
you . . .

Celebrate your good times with an album of firsts. Leave spaces next to photos of your first date, first Christmas, first vacation, first time white-water rafting, and first anniversary to add poems, prose, letters, and other memories.

SNAP YOUR ART OUT

Photography is perhaps the most accessible way of producing personalized art. Most of us haven't the time, talent, or inclination to take up watercolor painting, learn to blow a trumpet, or throw a pot (except in anger); yet becoming an arty photographer is within everyone's grasp. We suggest you set out to create photo-art that stimulates you both emotionally as well as visually. Whether you want to become monochrome magicians, specializing in moody black-and-white portraits, or focus on composing stunning landscapes using saturated colors, there are people, books, camera clubs, and gear to get you there.

PICTURE THIS

Many people fantasize about being cover models. Take some dramatic portraits of your partner to rediscover subtle curves and textures of his face and skin. Pros say the relationship between photographer and model is a crucial component of a completed work of art. So poor rapport means poor pics. If your partner feels ill at ease or overexposed, take time to unwind together and persuade him to let his personality shine. If you stimulate poise at a photo shoot, it will build trust in other areas. Time taken here isn't wasted. The sensitivity and perception you show will spill over into the rest of your relationship. Find something about your partner that you love and focus on it. It might be her long hair, her bedroom eyes, or that look. Take turns being sitter and snapper, or snuggle up for some couple shots taken with a timer.

PRIVATE VIEWS

Slip a snap into a love note.
Lost for words? Check out
IDEA 1, Read 'em and weep.

Try
another
idea . . .

Of course, your interest in your partner is more
than merely aesthetic. Taking "glamour" shots,
exploring and capturing images of each other's
bodies from interesting angles, is a clandestine yet sensual pleasure. If,
photographically speaking, you're going all the way, you might need to go digital or
set up a home darkroom to develop your indecent exposures.

CLUB TOGETHER

Camera clubs are great places for couples to improve skills; you can learn how to
use your flashy new equipment and look at the world from alternative angles. The
ones we've been to are full of helpful enthusiasts eager to pass on a lifetime of
experience (sometimes overly eager!). Socializing with other couples who share your
passion is a surefire way of making friends.

PINUPS

Albums are great, but we never look at them
often enough. Why not surround yourself with
a few of your memories? Try a photo wall
where you rehang regularly, gallery style, or peg
a few new prints along a simple clothesline
pulled taut across a bare wall.

"A photo is a reprieve, an act
of suspension, a charm. If
you see something terrible or
wonderful, that you can't
take in or focus on, take a
picture of it, hold the camera
to it. Look again when it's
safe."
GRAHAM SWIFT, author

Defining
idea . . .

181

OFFSHOOTS

By printing photos onto special computer paper, you can transfer your favorites onto T-shirts, mugs, mouse pads, and other household items. Imagine your partner's face when he discovers you've snuck a personalized T-shirt into his luggage when he's on a business trip. That way he can still go to bed with you, even if you're apart.

How did it go?

Q   We thought taking suggestive photos would be a turn-on. It wasn't. My wife, Mirabelle, complained that I made her look like the Michelin Man and went to bed in tears. According to the saying, the camera never lies, but couldn't it just fib a little?

A   *Oh, dear. We suggest you go all out and treat her to a full makeover and photo shoot with a professional photographer—you'll be amazed at the results. And if you go along, you could pick up some of his tricks of the trade.*

Q   My partner's a model. He's been photographed by pros all over the world. I can't compete with that. What can I do instead?

A   *Leave figurative stuff to them and concentrate on making some magical landscapes together. Once you've snapped some perfect rolling hills, crashing waves, or serene sunsets, have one blown up onto a canvas and hang it over your bed.*

42

Making a splash

Water, water everywhere and not all of it's to drink. Relationship feeling parched? Make the most of the revitalizing properties of H$_2$O. Use it or watch it disappear down the drain.

We want you to come clean. When was the last time you and your partner took a bath or shower together, when you washed her hair or scrubbed his back?

COME CLEAN

Think back to those early months, perhaps in his apartment or your first home together. Remember those times you'd spend together in the bath or shower? A Sunday morning slowly lathering your lover with soap or body wash, carefully rinsing suds away before toweling her down. Some people say we love baths and feel comforted by them because of the feeling of returning to the womb. One thing's for sure, warm water stimulates the release of those feel-good endorphins that induce a natural high. It also opens up your blood vessels, an important first step to enhanced sensual pleasure. Good clean fun in the bathroom is not the

Here's an idea for you . . .

Share a bath with your partner tonight. Fluff up some towels in the dryer, fill your bathroom with candles, and chill your best bottle of white. Add a few drops of musk-scented oils to the bathwater if you like, but leave your lavender bath salts on the windowsill. Mr. Right doesn't want to go to work smelling like someone's granny.

exclusive territory of the recently coupled, and the sooner you can start scrubbing your partner up the better.

WASHFUL THINKING

Back in the fifties and sixties, couples going through a difficult patch would be advised to wash the family car together (nowadays, it's more a question of which one?). Most must have been baffled at this suggestion: what on earth had this to do with relationship repair? But it works. It helps in a number of ways. There isn't a natural hierarchy for car washing. You have to work together. Couples are likely to work in a companionable silence initially, doing different tasks, before showing off "their" shiny chrome or fooling around while buffing bodywork. But what really makes this exercise different from other household chores is working outside with buckets of soapy water. It sounds banal, but we often forget just how much fun playing with water is. And it's so difficult to stay angry or sulky with your partner if you're both making fools of yourselves with water fights, hoses, buckets, and sponges. And you get a clean car at the end of it. And you'll have to get out of your wet clothes and towel each other down.

Defining idea . . .

"Wash me in the water
Where you wash your dirty
daughter
And I shall be whiter
Than the whitewash on the
wall."
The Top of the Dixie, song from World War I

MAKE WAVES

Water is an important part of most couples' summer vacations. Think of the laughs you have in the sea, swimming, rowing, playing volleyball in the hotel pool, water-skiing, white-water rafting, or surfing. But why stop there? Officials who put up the "No petting" signs at municipal pools know a thing or two about public baths and private passions. Plunge into a pool and swim with your partner. Make it a regular date.

GOOD VIBRATIONS

Once the privilege of the seriously rich, you'll find a Jacuzzi or hot tub in most spas, and in many hotels and gyms. What a great way to re-energize tired bodies. Once those aching limbs have been refreshed, a little surreptitious footsie will get your love life back on its feet. Need more convincing? All those bubbles give you a toning massage so your body will be in top form for any after-pool parties for two.

LETTING OFF STEAM

Hot saunas and balmy steam rooms are great places to lounge with your beloved. Add a few drops of sensual rose oil or sandalwood to really sizzle things up. And learn a lesson from those sexy Swedes: hold hands and jump out of the heat into an ice-cold shower for the ultimate passion boost.

Wondering whether to suggest a quickie in the shower? Check out IDEA 38, *Sex*.

Try another idea...

"Consider bathing or showering together or use the bathroom as a venue for sex. The combination of water, body wash, and slippery skin is highly erotic. If you choose not to actually make love in the bathroom, a warm bath before sex will help you relax and put you in a sensual mood."
JULIA COLE, relationship therapist

Defining idea...

"Save water—shower with a friend."
GRAFFITI

Defining idea...

How did
it go?

Q I used to go swimming a lot and would love to swim with my wife. Unfortunately, Amina can't swim, and would feel self-conscious going to lessons. I reckon it would be a great thing to do together, but how can I persuade her to join in?

A *Why not go and hang out in the Jacuzzi together first? If it overlooks the pool, even better, as you'll be able to show Amina what she's missing. Once you've whetted her appetite, ask at your local pool about intensive swimming lessons for adults. Many swimming pools hold women-only swimming lessons, which might make her less self-conscious.*

Q Whenever we take a bath together I'm always squashed up at the tap end, with the faucet digging into my back. I also can't reach the soap. I know we could swap ends sometimes, but I'm old-fashioned and chivalrous, and feel it's my duty to suffer on her behalf. Is there a way around this?

A *In the short term, we suggest you both face the same direction in the bath, with your feet pointing toward the faucet. By leaning back into your partner you miss out on eye contact, but it still gives you enough room for a warm, wet cuddle. In the long term, you need a traditional-style bath to match your commendable attitude. A deep bath with faucets in the middle rather than at either end is what is called for.*

43

Cheap thrills

Relationship repair often means spending big bucks. Everyone knows going out keeps relationships fun, but you don't have to blow a fortune to blow the cobwebs out of your life.

Showing your partner she means the world to you doesn't need to cost a bundle. Once you know how, it's easy to show your lover a good time without busting your budget.

FREE FOR ALL

There may be no such thing as a free lunch, but many re-energizing fun days and flirty nights are free. When was the last time you held hands and went walking at sunset or in the morning? Or played hide-and-seek? Or truth or dare? Time to make a list of things you've always wanted to know about your other half but never dared ask: think up some steamy forfeits and enjoy a night in with a difference. For an adrenaline surge, take your partner for a spin in her fantasy car. Glam up, visit a swanky showroom, and ask for a test drive. Once you've got a taste of the high life,

Here's an idea for you . . .

The key to lasting love may be on your doorstep. Play hometown tourists. Raid your nearest tourist office for free maps and leaflets about local attractions. Get out there to see your neighborhood—and each other—in a better light.

you might like to try the outing we call Penthouse Sweet. Dress like millionaires, adopt assumed names, and make appointments with out-of-town real estate agents to see dream properties in exclusive areas. Upmarket viewers are often provided with complimentary champagne . . .

DRAMA QUEENS (AND KINGS)

Want to add some drama to your relationship but can't afford a babysitter and dinner on top of high-price theater tickets? Matinees are often half price, and if the kids are at school you won't need a babysitter. If evenings are your only option, university drama departments often put on reduced-rate performances for the public. Students on their summer break? Try a play-reading evening at home instead. A two-person script might be a good starting point, or pair up with other couples to form a play-reading circle. Once you've found your voice, join a local amateur dramatic group and join in the action.

GET CRAFTY

Many artists and craftspeople have open days and other free events in their studios. Find out through local art schools, libraries, or craft councils. We love watching our local glassblowers, and enjoy bargain hunting in their sales. Feeling inspired? Have creative evenings in: make a mosaic mirror, write a short story, paint a mural in the back garden, teach the cat to crochet . . .

LESSONS IN LOVE

Swap skills. Teach him how to change a tire and get him to show you how to waltz. The student–teacher dynamic is powerful and guaranteed to add oomph to your love life.

TEN CHEAP AND CHEERFUL DATES

- Have an art house or blockbuster movie night. Rent the first film you watched together, make mountains of microwave popcorn, and turn your sofa into the back row.
- Rent a tandem bicycle and explore. Life is sweet when you're on the seats of a bicycle made for two. Add panache with an inexpensive cheese, bread, and wine picnic.
- Eat at home but go out afterward for dessert and coffee in a swanky restaurant. Share an ice cream sundae and let her have the cherry.
- Rendezvous in an exclusive hotel. You don't need to book a room, just put on your finery and people-watch in the foyer. Drinks may be pricey, so just buy one and enjoy complimentary nibbles.

Try another idea...

Cherish your cheap date memories by snapping with a disposable camera. Camera shy? You won't be after reading IDEA 41, *Snap, cackle, and print.*

Defining idea...

"Free love? As if love is anything but free. Man has bought brains, but all the millions in the world have failed to buy love."
EMMA GOLDMAN, Russian-born anarchist

- Drive down memory lane. Take a tour of places that have special memories: where you went on your first date, had your first kiss, proposed, your favorite restaurant or view, wherever makes your hearts beat faster.
- Hunt down her favorite author and surprise her with a visit to a book signing. Bookshops advertise forthcoming events, but to find out what her author has planned, contact the publisher directly.
- Serve your partner breakfast in bed with a themed twist. For a French breakfast, put on some accordion music and serve hot coffee and *pain au chocolat*. French maid's outfits and mustaches optional. French kisses, on the other hand, are just a serving suggestion.
- Put stars in his eyes. Borrow a book on astronomy from your local library, pitch a tent in the garden, and teach him about stargazing.
- Grab some culture. Many museums, art galleries, and exhibitions are free. It also pays to hunt out smaller, specialty places as they're often more intimate.
- Drop in on an open mic night at a comedy club. As this is where new acts cut their teeth, you won't see any famous faces, but what a thrill to see someone before they were famous.

Defining idea...

"Money is what you'd get on beautifully without if only other people weren't so crazy about it."
MARGARET CASE HARRIMAN

Q These low-cost and cheerful outings are great, but my missus already thinks I'm cheap (okay, I am) and your suggestions will only confirm it. Any better (but still cheap) suggestions?

A *Why not sell these ideas as extra treats rather than replacements. The odd, expensive bunch of roses wouldn't go amiss, either.*

Q I'm eager to dress up and do some of the daring things you suggest. Unfortunately my partner gets anxious and worries we'll get into trouble. How can I allay his fears?

A *Start small and work your way up. The object is to have fun, not to induce anxiety. Having said that, overcoming something that makes you anxious is more fun than fun.*

How did it go?

191

44

We can work it out

Spending so little time together that you barely recognize your partner? Working with your other half might be the answer.

Imagine a partner who understands your job perfectly, appreciates the stresses, shares your ambitions and achievements, and just knows when it's been a bad day in the office...

Frank and Sharon Barnett, experts on enterpreneurial couples, call couples in business together "copreneurs." At their best, copreneurs enjoy shared power, joint decision making, and better conflict resolution. Coworking couples are less likely to miss each other during the day or grow apart over time. When they both feel responsible for work-related success, there's less envy and they enjoy a more harmonious relationship.

Friends often express surprise when we tell them our relationship is improved by working together. When we rave about our latest venture, we get comments like "We could never do that. We'd end up arguing." And remarks like this come from couples doing a fantastic and difficult job bringing up three very different kids.

Here's an idea for you . . .

Already working with your partner and wondering how it can give your relationship more zest? Learn to treat your partner as a trusted colleague.

. . . and another

Pulling rank or expecting favors at work will end in tears or resentment. Once you accept that your work and home relationships are different, your partnership will take off in a new direction.

Our work is the cornerstone of our relationship. The old dog learns new tricks from the younger cat and she picks his brain for the sort of stuff you'd otherwise only gain from experience. It provides a common interest with shared goals, and it's great fun. Lots of couples ask us our secret. It's simple. There are five rules we live and work by:

- Keep work-related things out of your bedroom and at least one other room. Snuggling up over *Bluff Your Way in Advanced Electronic Circuits* might set sparks flying one night, but in the long run it's a turn-off.
- Respect each other's different work styles. Maybe she's "boom or bust" and you're more "slow and steady," but as long as you get the job done, who cares? If it annoys you, try using humor. Teasing comments like "Last to finish buys dinner" is more effective than "Why don't you ever pull your weight, you idle, slimy toad?"
- Sometimes you will need to work late, but set a usual "finish time" to demarcate home and work. Do something domestic at quitting time. We often walk to the supermarket or plan an evening out.
- Identify at least one evening each week when you don't discuss work. Despite your best efforts, some shop talk will inevitably spill over into home time, but you should still be able to focus on other areas of your relationship.
- Have separate work and play wardrobes. You're much more likely to talk about work if you're wearing a business suit to do the dishes. When you take off your work clothes at the end of the day, imagine peeling off your work-self. Sounds like psychobabble, but it's surprisingly effective.

Nat and Betty revamped their working lives and relationship. Their day starts early. When it's still dark, they can be found selecting fruit and vegetables from the wholesale market. Then they're off to whatever market they're selling at. Nat used to be a plumber and Betty worked a couple of mornings as a classroom assistant. "This way we see a lot more of each other," says Betty. "Nat has always worked hard. He rarely used to get home before seven and on weekends we'd get emergency calls when people were flooded. Now we're a double act," she continues. "He's a funny guy who flirts with old ladies. He only gets away with it because I'm there laughing at his quips." Nat finds they get along better since he changed jobs: "I used to have a liquid lunch and maybe a few beers on my way home. When I got in, Betty was always cross with me. We sometimes go for a drink together now, but not often as I don't feel nearly as stressed."

Living to work or working to live? What are you waiting for? Is there a joint passion you can exploit? If your accountant gives your business plan short shrift, why not give it a go for one day a week?

Having the opposite problem and seeing too much of your partner? Time to develop some interests he doesn't share. Check out IDEA 23, *All by myself*.

Try another idea..... .

"Working with someone you love creates the feeling of working as one."
MARCIA MCDOUGAL, artisan who works with her husband, Bruce

Defining idea...

"Working together is like one plus one equals three."
DUB JAMES, who coruns Boomer House Books from home with his wife, Janet

Defining idea . . .

How did
it go?

Q **I took a job as a secretary at my husband's office. I thought we'd be able to see more of each other and improve our relationship. It hasn't. I had no idea how unpopular he was at work and I find myself siding with the other girls. At five o'clock they get away from the boss yet I have to drive home with him. I sometimes can't help bringing up office issues, but this just ruins the evening. What can I do?**

A *Short of asking for a transfer, we suggest you keep the home/office divide as big as possible. Why not arrange to go home separately or, if that's not practical, make a rule not to talk shop outside work? Maybe you're siding with other secretaries because you don't want to be seen as the boss's pet. But if there are genuine problems at work, we suggest you address them there, rather than at home, and during work hours. You might be able to improve things for everybody. By sorting out this work-related problem, you'll learn useful lessons that you can apply to domestic arguments, too.*

Q **My wife and I run a small shop together. It was fine for the first three or four years, but business has been getting a lot harder since a supermarket opened a few miles down the road. The stress is really getting to us and we are finding it hard to switch it off. What's the answer?**

A *Rather than worrying about the business, you need to talk about options in light of the new competition. You will have to make some hard choices or else you could lose everything. See what professional advice you can get and act on it. Good luck.*

45

Who's laughing now?

Crying over the state of your relationship? Feeling angry, hurt, or bored? Looking for a love potion to zap stress and take the bite out of bickering? Laughter's the best medicine.

For repairing a relationship, laughter is seriously strong stuff. It relieves tension, lowers blood pressure, strengthens your immune system, and gives your brain a boost to help you remember birthdays, anniversaries, and other vital statistics.

A LAUGH A DAY KEEPS SEPARATION AT BAY

In the trade, we talk about defense mechanisms. Just a fancy name for the ways we all distort reality to cope with stressful circumstances. Some defense mechanisms are bad news: there's projection (blaming someone else), denial (not me!), regression (having temper tantrums when you're forty-five), rationalization (I wasn't really being unfaithful, I was just seeing how far I could put my tongue down her throat). This is also an example of a bad joke. Sigmund Freud, who knew a bit about this sort of thing, believed humor was one of the most useful defense.

197

Here's an idea for you . . .

What are you waiting for? Laugh at a funny book, chuckle at a DVD of _The Simpsons_, or go to a comedy club and strut your stuff at an open mic session. It doesn't matter how you get your laughs, just get out there and giggle.

mechanisms going if used at the right moments. If you can make a joke out of a problem, you feel in control. Make a crack about the president or your father-in-law, and for that split second you won't feel so oppressed and can hopefully cheer up your beloved. After all, if it's stressing you, it's probably affecting your partner.

GRIN AND BEAR IT

Remember, this isn't about snickering at your partner as she tries to shoehorn herself into a size six sundress three days after giving birth to triplets, but rather laughing together when fate deals you a bad hand. If you can laugh at your troubles, they stop being threatening and become something you can take on together. A sense of humor gives you and your partner a positive perspective. If you can whistle "Singin' in the Rain" while your roof leaks, it becomes a challenge rather than a catastrophe. If your girlfriend is stressed out by her picky boss, why not do some funny impressions of him? Still skeptical? Let's try to put it another way. Laughter is a great physical stress buster. Even a quick chuckle loosens tense jaw and shoulder muscles. Experts have discovered that laughter lowers cortisol levels while raising levels of T-lymphocytes. "Oh good," we hear you say. "I was hoping that would happen." Well, you should, because this means that having a laugh boosts your immune system. Which is good news, as stress weakens it, leaving you run down and vulnerable to bugs.

HAVIN' A LAUGH

Laughing is probably the last thing on your mind when an argument's brewing, but it's probably when you most need to. When it's hard to see the funny side, see if you can make a humorous observation, especially about yourself. Laughing together instead of quarreling improves communication and puts difficulties into perspective.

Laughing in the face of problems gives you energy to come up with zany solutions. Humor releases pent-up creativity and helps you think laterally.

Used laughter to diffuse a heated argument? Fantastic. For other ways to cope when the going gets tough, see **IDEA 13, *Stormy weather.***

Try another idea.....

"If you have only one smile in you, give it to the people you love. Don't be surly at home, then go out in the street and start grinning 'Good morning' at total strangers."
MAYA ANGELOU

Defining idea...

Observational comedians are as bright as buttons and razor sharp. See them on so-called serious TV shows and they can take most professional politicians apart. How? They have developed ways of looking at the world, people, and problems differently, and are able to react in funny, off-the-wall ways. They often explore the gaps between how things are and how they are supposed to be. They've also found ways of remaining levelheaded under pressure and their solutions, which might seem daft, often contain constructive alternatives.

"If you can laugh at it, you can survive it."
BILL COSBY

Defining idea...

199

GAME FOR A LAUGH

Comedy clubs are light-years away from the old clubs with middle-aged stand-ups in bow ties with crappy routines of misogynistic and mother-in-law material. The clubs we go to and the people we have seen suggest that we are in the middle of a golden period of comedy. There are enough brilliant acts and original material to justify the claim that comedy is the new rock and roll. Even if you haven't heard of the comedians on the bill, you're sure to be in for a good night. Just don't sit too near the front. A trip to a comedy club, like a night at the opera, is one you'll never forget.

How did it go?

Q **I don't feel very happy at the moment, so taking my partner to a comedy club is the last thing I feel like doing. Why should I bother to make an effort?**

A *Our thoughts, our feelings, and what we do are all interrelated. Of course if you're happy, you're more likely to feel like going out to have a great night and think your relationship is amazing. But it works the other way, too. If you force yourself to have a laugh when you're feeling glum, you won't be miserable for long. Try it and your partner will thank you.*

Q **We have big financial worries. Our debt is just not funny. How can we laugh about it?**

A *Laughter will probably help you and your relationship survive monstrous money problems. As doctors and rescue workers know, dark humor has a lot going for it. Laughing in the face of debt stops you from feeling like victims.*

46

Walk the talk

When all else has failed, where can you turn? You could call in the pros who know what makes couples tick and are willing to work wonders for you.

Couples therapy might seem extreme, but a little expert help can fuel your own efforts to reignite that elusive spark.

We know that re-energizing your relationship can feel like hard work sometimes. Perhaps when you first met you were both full of hopes and expectations. Often, when we get to know our partners a bit better, we feel massively disappointed that they are not the combined sex goddess, gourmet chef, and superbrain all-in-one that we took them for.

While we'd agree that arguments and differences are part of all relationships, we'd also concur that when couples get stuck facing the same problems over and over, therapy can be a great opportunity.

Here's an idea for you . . . **Unsure whether couples therapy will help you? Why not investigate and ask for an assessment session? This'll give you a taste of what to expect and you'll have an idea of whether you and your partner will be able to trust and get along with the therapist.**

IT'S GOOD TO TALK

Ask yourself if any of these ring true for you:

- We don't talk anymore.
- He/she doesn't listen to me.
- We argue all the time.
- I'm not getting what I want from this relationship anymore.
- We can't agree on how to bring up the children.
- We disagree a lot about money.

Most of these statements will resonate with anyone in a relationship. But if you've been struggling to sort them out and are getting more and more frustrated or unhappy, a good therapist could have a profound effect on your relationship, salvaging treasures from what seemed like a wreck. They do this by helping you talk and, perhaps more important, listen to each other. Therapists working with couples know a relationship is intricate and complicated. They aren't like football referees or judges. Pros won't take sides or try to blame one of you. They'll chip in so that you can understand both yourself and your partner better.

WHAT GOES ON?

Forget all those images of men in white coats and padded cells. You won't have to lie on a couch or look for strange images in inkblots either. Instead you'll meet a skilled professional to chat about both your opinions and feelings. Be prepared for a lot of questions, though. Therapists will ask you probing questions to establish what problems you're facing and how you both see them. They'll need to know about how you met and the story of your relationship so far, and they'll also ask about the previous relationships you've both had. Sounds really nosy, doesn't it?

Couples often come to therapy after an affair has been discovered or confessed. Done the dirty? Find out how to make amends in IDEA 29, Unbreak my heart.

Try another idea . . .

They need to know this stuff to really understand what makes you both tick, individually and as a couple. Once they've gotten you figured out, they'll be able to help you understand yourself and your partner better, decide what you'd both like to change, and discuss how you can both make it happen.

TIME AND PLACE

Do you ever catch yourself mid-argument and think, "What are we actually fighting about?" It's common. The reason behind your door slamming or plate smashing might not be obvious. Pros can lend a hand by helping you both spot core problems and deal with them. Matt and Elaine spent months arguing about whose turn it was to take out the trash, wash the dishes, do the laundry, or feed the cat. In therapy they discovered that the real reason they were fighting so much was over money. Matt felt insecure because he earned a lot less than Elaine, who was fed up with supporting him and envious of her better-off friends.

If you're not sure why you and your partner quarrel all the time or get on each other's nerves, it might be time to call the experts. Therapy offers time in a place away from the

"When David [Arquette] and I got engaged, we started therapy together. I'd heard that the first year of marriage is the hardest, so we decided to work through all that stuff early."
COURTENEY COX

Defining idea . . .

203

normal stresses of daily living, giving you a chance to sit back and discover what has really been going on and what you need to tackle. He or she (and often one of each) will bring fresh ears and eyes to your relationship, as well as a wealth of expertise about what makes couples tick. Top themes in couples therapy are communication, finances, sex, and parenting. That said, you don't have to be in trouble to call in an expert. Lots of couples use time with a pro to improve their relationships.

How did it go?

Q **We've been investigating expert help and are unsure about the difference between couples therapy and sex therapy. Can you enlighten us?**

A *Sure. Couples therapy looks at all aspects of your relationship, while sex therapy focuses exclusively on sexual problems. Many relationship problems will have an effect on other areas, so sex might well come up during couples therapy.*

Q **I think therapy would help us, but we've heard it's expensive. We are not loaded with money—in fact, that may be our problem. Can we afford it?**

A *It's cheaper than getting divorced. Seriously, some therapists charge according to what you can pay, on a sliding scale. If this still works out to be too expensive, you might like to see a student therapist, who would work with you and your partner under supervision.*

47

I've got you under my skin

Remember when you first met, your partner could do no wrong? Chances are that his little quirks and foibles, once so endearing, have become irritating.

Change is possible, but you'll have to start close to home. We'll help you live happily with a lover who farts at the dinner table or who chews her toenails in bed.

Love may be blind, but infatuation is deaf. When Nilesh first met Luke, everything he said was attractive, amorous, or hilarious. But recently Nilesh has grown tired of the same old jokes and they have started to become irritating. When we're first attracted to our partners, it's often because they are our opposite in various ways. Fun-loving Felix fell in love with timid Therese. She admired him, and sometimes wishes she could be a bit more outgoing, like he is. But that's just not how she is, and sometimes his loudness gets on her nerves. At the same time, he feels annoyed that she often wimps out of his social whirl.

Remember the Greek myth about Procrustes? You don't? Well he was the thief with an iron bed. When he invited people to sleep in it, Procrustes expected them to fit his bed perfectly. Too short? He had them stretched. Too tall? He cut their legs off.

Here's an idea for you . . .

Fold a piece of paper in half. On one side, write down half a dozen things you'd love to change about your partner. On the other, list how you can change your response or reaction to each of them. If you shout every time she leaves the top off the toothpaste, try humming instead. Sick of swearing when he leaves the toilet seat up? Smile instead. Practice makes perfect.

Many of us make a metaphorical Procrustean bed for our partners, trying to change them to fit our own measures.

We understand there are things about your partner that you'd like to change; we've yet to meet anyone without eccentricities or flaws. But while there's no magic pill or potion to alter or modify your mate (not yet, anyway), you can transform how you react to his or her irritations, revolutionizing your relationship. It takes time to learn to compromise and accommodate. But relationships are not static—for better or worse, they change. And you can change with them.

Take John and Meredith. "John farts at the dinner table," complains Meredith, who is fed up. But what happens if we turn this statement around: Meredith allows herself to be annoyed by John farting at the dinner table. Changing the onus removes blame and opens a door for change. If, like Meredith, there's something you really can't live with, tell your partner.

Be cautious though, as constant criticism corrodes couple harmony, so only enlighten him once and make a point of noticing next time he does something kind or loving. When you tell your partner of an irritation, it's essential to avoid holding him responsible, as that only encourages defensiveness. It's also important to explain why it annoys you.

So, instead of Meredith saying "You selfish fool, farting away frenziedly. It's typical of you to be so disrespectful," she tried this: "I don't like it when you fart during dinner because the smell makes me lose my appetite." Starting her appeal with "I" takes the spotlight off John, making him more likely to listen to her. If she finds out what she does that annoys John and makes an effort to curb it, they're both on to a winner.

Sometimes we get under each others' skin when we're feeling jaded, tired, or fed up. Take some time out for yourself and recharge. See IDEA 23, *All by myself*.

Try another idea . . .

TIME TRAVEL

Cast your mind back to your courtship. Try to recall how you felt about her annoying quirk then. Write down what you liked about it, how it made you feel inside, and what it made you feel about her. Ben did this exercise and was able to feel less exasperated about his partner Bronwen's toenail chewing. "I had forgotten that I used to think it was quite kooky, disinhibited, and unconventional. Although I still don't like it, I've realized that it's those qualities I love about Bron. If she used nail clippers, she'd be a different person. Her chewing doesn't bother me in the same way."

"The sound of her slurping her jelly, which he had hoped that just this once she would spare him, made him see how husbands murdered their wives."
From "Lately," by HANIF KUREISHI

Defining idea . . .

207

How did
it go?

Q **My husband served in the army for twenty-three years and complains that I don't keep the house tidy enough for him. I've never worked so hard in my life! However, I'm not sure I can, or want to, keep it up forever. What should I do?**

A *There's no need to become a martyr to somebody else's cause. Be assertive and set a limit on the amount of housework you're prepared to do each week. Suggest that if it still doesn't come up to his standards, he pays for a cleaner or scrubs the floors himself.*

Q **I used to love Monique's French accent. Increasingly it has been getting to me. She's lived in this country for fifteen years and her mispronunciations just aren't sexy anymore. I know it's my problem, but I feel irritable every time she speaks. What can I do to keep it from getting to me?**

A *Monique comes as a package. Maybe along with her accent there is brilliant French cuisine or a Gallic gift in the bedroom? If you try to associate her accent with these positive qualities it won't seem so annoying.*

48

Domestic detox

Why do most men do most of the driving? And most women most of the housework? Have you carved out roles for yourselves, and now feel stuck? Review your chores and renew your romance.

At the beginning of your relationship did you sit down and decide who was going to take out the trash every Wednesday evening? Vacuum the living room? Cook Sunday dinner?

Did you ever agree that one or the other of you would drive the bulk of the long-distance car trips or always sort out the tickets for airline bookings? No, we didn't either. Yet in most relationships, we find ourselves committed to being the only person doing a particular task. Maybe you get stuck with taking out the cat litter because your partner always spills it on the carpet. (Have you ever asked yourself why that happens?) Perhaps you do all the long-distance driving because it's what the man is "supposed" to do. Or do you care more than your partner that the bookcases are dusted and the fridge is cleaned regularly? Some of us can't live with a blown lightbulb while our partners aren't too bothered.

"If I don't wash the car nobody will," whines Nick. It's a source of festering discontent and resentment. He feels it's just not fair. His partner Alice has grumbles

Here's an idea for you . . .

Have a short household meeting at the start of each week. Write down all the cleaning, shopping, fetching, collecting, and other errands that need to be done and split them up. We find it helps to write each partner's initials by their jobs. Put the list up somewhere prominent, like on the fridge or kitchen bulletin board. And don't mention it again during the week. There's no uglier utterance than nagging. Some people like to get their jobs out of the way and feel smug about it. Others are last-minute merchants. As long as everything gets done, who cares?

Defining idea . . .

"Hatred of domestic work is a natural and admirable result of civilization."
REBECCA WEST

of her own: Why should one particular partner be stuck washing their dirty laundry and making sure that the household doesn't run out of toilet paper or toothpaste?

TIMES THEY ARE A CHANGIN'

Most men have discovered that cooking, especially if you don't have to do it all the time, is actually quite therapeutic. It's a great way to unwind at the end of the week or after a hard day at the office. Chopping onions is a great method of getting rid of pent-up anger or aggression, and putting meals together is actually fun. Conversely, more and more women are doing home-repair tasks and getting deep satisfaction from wallpapering, tiling, and painting—once the exclusive preserve of the males of the tribe. Better still, many couples have come to realize that cooking or even tidying up hardly feels like a chore when the two of you are tackling it together. The work is done in half the time, leaving you both with spare time to do all that stuff you really want to do.

NOBODY WEARS THE PANTS

In a lot of long-term partnerships, one member suffers from what we call "victim-of-your-own-success syndrome." One partner always reads maps or does the big drives because he—sorry, but it usually is a he—is better at it than she is.

Of course he is: he's put in the mileage. But if you share the job around, her second best can easily become joint equal. When a lover's self-esteem is built on being the sole role-holder, he might find it difficult to let go. When your partner has a go at what is traditionally your job, avoid being critical or sniping if at first he doesn't measure up—neither did you when you first started.

While you're thinking about your home, why not look at IDEA 27, *Dump your junk*, to find ways to make it more manageable?

Try another idea . . .

"Keeping house is as unpleasant and filthy as coal mining and the pay's a lot worse."
P. J. O'ROURKE

Defining idea . . .

"Conran's Law of Housework— it expands to fill the time available plus half an hour."
SHIRLEY CONRAN, writer of *Superwoman*

Defining idea . . .

Q **An out-of-town superstore has just been built. My husband drives me there for our weekly shopping and drives me crazy once we get there. He wants to take over the job and tell me how to do what I've been doing unnoticed for the past seventeen years! Why should I put up with it?**

A *That's men for you. Seriously, you could suggest that he goes alone a couple of times, or you could suggest that you divide the list into two: you could get the meat and vegetables one week while he gets the household goods and other odds and ends, then reverse it next time.*

Q **I would truly love to share the housework with my partner but she seems unable to do the simplest thing without breaking something. Is there an evening class for this sort of thing?**

A *It's a nice thought! Seriously, she's either doing it on purpose to get out of doing the housework or she's just naturally very clumsy. Don't assume it's the former as she may have a condition called dyspraxia, which would explain her butterfingers. We suggest you both make a list of the household tasks and odd jobs that each of you hates. You may well find that what you hate, she might stomach. If you both hate the same jobs, or if the breakages continue, it might be cheaper to pay a cleaner or a relationship counselor.*

Q **My husband always hangs the toilet paper the wrong way, so the paper faces inward instead of outward. It makes me so irritated. I've shown him lots of times. Why is he so difficult?**

A *There's no easy way to tell you this, but it's your problem, not his. If it's that important to you, hang it yourself.*

49

Sowing the seeds of love

Put some spring into the autumn years of your relationship. We'll help you sow, hoe, and prune your way to blossoming passion. Nurture your garden and nurture your love life.

Does your closeness with your lover wax and wane? Relationships have seasons, and a bit of joint gardening can teach you how to make the most of love's summer and weather the worst.

SECRET GARDEN

A bit of joint gardening is time together well spent: You might think it's about achieving a common goal, but gardening is so much more than that. Like many couples, your garden may well be used by the whole family, with different areas for entertaining, growing edibles, and playing. We recommend you select a spot that you both can convert into a hideaway from the rest of the world—a backdrop for midday musings, moonlight picnics, and tussling behind the bushes.

Here's an idea for you . . .

Hammocks are great to hang out in, but for the ultimate sensual seat, you need a chamomile bed. It's easy to grow one by planting chamomile in a low raised bed. Fill your bed with soil mixed with ericaceous compost. We suggest you plant pot-grown chamomile plants about 4 inches apart, in March to May. Once your bed has filled out a bit, just add a couple of pillows. The chamomile will release its fragrance every time you use your bed. Keep it well watered in summer and trim it often.

Lovers' gardens should ooze serenity. Your perfect spot will be secluded, but also soft and soothing. You might opt for a wildflower meadow with poppies and grasses, or something more formal with lawn and borders. Talk to each other about colors. Do you want something bright and bold, or would you prefer romantic hues like pinks, violets, and muted blues? Plants with intense fragrance, like lilies, rose, jasmine, and honeysuckle, are relaxing and can send you to sleep. If you'd prefer a love garden that energizes and refreshes, plant herbs like lemon thyme, peppermint, and rosemary.

HEDGE YOUR BETS

Surround your area with hedges, fencing, a trellis, or other screens. It can be particularly effective to paint a trellis before growing climbing roses and passion flowers up it. Accessorize with wind chimes, water features, and hammocks, or hang a swing from a tree. If you're feeling adventurous, why not build a tree house with turrets and a drawbridge? If you have children, you might have to build two, otherwise your love nest will soon be their playhouse.

SPRING

In the spring of your romance, you probably felt high on love. You may have even lost your appetite. This is because the appetite-suppressing chemical phenylethylamine is released when we fall in love. Spring is also a good time for romance in your garden. Recall your early heady days as you bask in sweet smells of lavender, rose, or lily of the valley. Feast on an outdoor picnic under a rose arch. Or get raunchy behind the rhododendrons. Focus on the structures underpinning your relationship as you build structures in your garden, like an arbor or a love seat.

Backyard shed depressingly full of rubbish? Clear out the clutter and clear up trouble in your relationship. See IDEA 27, *Dump your junk.*

Try another idea . . .

"Let us be grateful to people who make us happy, they are the charming gardeners who make our souls blossom."
MARCEL PROUST

Defining idea . . .

SUMMER

In the summer of love, we produce higher levels of two other hormones, called oxytocin and vasopresin. Both bring out your nesting instinct. A radical garden makeover at this time could give you both a joint focus. Oxytocin has been called the touch hormone. Increase oxytocin levels by touching each other and your plants. Textures have never been more important in your corner of paradise. Include plants you can stroke, like pussy willow and pampas grasses, which have sensual feathery fronds. Poppies are papery and delicate. Lilies feel silky smooth and sexy.

AUTUMN

In your garden, as in your relationship, autumn is a time of change. Traditionally the time of the so-called seven-year itch, maybe you're longing for a bit of instant gratification. Sometimes love can't wait, and gardens are no different. There's not much point planning a garden that will be a sensual Eden in a couple of years but a barren desert until then. So don't be tempted to grow everything from seed. And while you're waiting for the passion flowers to climb, enjoy some pink and red annuals.

WINTER

Relationships often suffer from winter blues: times when everything feels dormant and the world looks bleak. The winter of love can make your relationship feel a little sloth-like. So get out there. Gardening lowers blood pressure and makes you feel upbeat. Browse thrift shops for alternative garden accessories. Could that rusty colander be painted and turned into a hanging basket? Share plans and joint visions. Growing together will help you get that spring honeymoon feeling back, but like composted soil, it'll be deeper and richer.

Defining idea...

"All really grim gardeners possess a good sense of humus."
R. J. YEATMAN, author of *Garden Rubbish*

Q   **I'm fed up with wasting weekends and vacations stuck in lines at our local garden center. I don't feel gardening is helping our relationship at all, as the only input my wife wants from me is to do all the heavy-duty stuff. How can I enjoy it more?**

How did it go?

A   *There's no reason why getting gardening supplies should take up all your free time. You need to make better use of modern technology. Find garden centers where you can order online or by telephone for home delivery. Pay a little more for others to do the fetching and carrying, and consider employing a local student to do the mundane jobs like lawn mowing. This'll free the two of you up to spend vacations out in the open, getting creative or visiting public gardens for inspiration.*

Q   **We made a beautiful chamomile bed and enjoyed lounging on it over the summer. But now that it's cooler, it's starting to look a little patchy. What can we do?**

A   *Chamomile beds do tend to get like that in winter. We suggest you fill the gaps next spring with a few new plants. Next year, take cuttings in the summer to fill any bald patches the following year.*

50

Come fly away

Relationships, like books, films, or plays, have a beginning, a middle, and an end. Need a hand navigating your way through the muddle in the middle?

Roughly 30 percent of marriages split up when couples are between forty and sixty. Why? Midlife crises, male menopause, empty nest syndrome, career catastrophes, wandering bifocals—Old Father Time has plenty of ways.

Too old for clubbing, too young for meals-on-wheels? All couples face times of turbulence: changes at home, at work, in our bodies, and in our minds. The middle years—of your life or your relationship—don't have to be heartbreaking or alarming. Use them as a catalyst. They're the power for change. Finally free from childcare, you're free to be what you want to be and probably have more disposable income than ever.

A mid-relationship crisis is a multifarious beast. Perhaps you've been dissatisfied with your relationship for a long time, and it feels like make-or-break time. Forty-seven-year-old Neil was kept awake at night fretting over missed opportunities, wondering what might have been if he'd accepted that job offer or married his

Here's an idea for you . . .

Next time you feel threatened or ground down by midlife or mid-relationship blues, try to see them as midlife opportunities. Challenge beliefs like "I'm no good for anything now that our children have all started school." Turn them into new openings, like "Now I have time to be what I've always wanted to be."

ex-girlfriend. He would brood silently for hours and gave his wife Elaine the cold shoulder. She shared his sadness and felt she'd never done what she wanted to either. Disappointment could have destroyed them, but they were able to turn it around. They moved out of the city, Elaine is retraining as a career counselor and Neil has taken a year's sabbatical to write the novel he's dreamed about for a decade. They're poorer financially, but pursuing their different life courses has made their relationship richer.

You don't have to be middle-aged to have a midlife crisis. Plenty of young people have spoken about their quarter-life crises and college students are blaming their relationship breakups on mid-university crises.

KEEP YOUR RELATIONSHIP PERT

Mid-relationship is a superb time for assessing and appraising your relationship. Sabina's dad Arif calls it "keeping it PERT." PERT is a project management technique he was taught years ago as a young accountant, but he swears it's the secret to his long and happy marriage. The original PERT was developed in the late fifties for the US Navy's Polaris project. Arif's is adapted for relationship rejuvenation and works like this:

Plan

So you woke up this morning and wanted to throw in the towel? It's surprisingly common to feel the need to destroy or give up all we've worked for. Many people think that if they just had a better, more understanding partner, all would be well again. But wait. Before you send that resignation letter, call in the divorce lawyers, or book a one-way ticket out of town, make a plan together. It sounds clichéd, but write down where you both want to be a year from now. Put it somewhere obvious, where you'll see it often—like stuck to your computer monitor or in your wallet. Now write twelve monthly targets that need to be done to meet your plan. Divide each into four weekly steps and set a weekly meeting to evaluate how things are going.

If your partner's in a rut, why not spoil him for a day? Check out IDEA 37, *What a difference a day makes.*

Try another idea . . .

Evaluate

Midlife provides a unique focus for change. As you look at your weekly plan, evaluate the progress you've made over the week and your relationship in general. You might find yourselves discovering aspects of your personalities you'd forgotten. By working together to achieve your plans, your relationship becomes richer and more satisfying.

Review Technique

Review your methods for reaching your year plan in light of your evaluation. Are they working? Do they fit in with the relationship you want? What alternatives are there?

"The greatest potential for growth and self-realization exists in the second half of life."
CARL JUNG, psychoanalyst

Defining idea . . .

Forty-two-year-old Norah took early retirement for health reasons the same month her partner Carl was promoted to the top job at his bank. She'd always been the higher earner and the power imbalance threatened their twenty-year relationship. Carl wanted to spend what he saw as his prime enjoying his money and status. It was hard coming home and caring for a sickly wife.

Let's follow Norah and Carl through a PERT. Carl's plan was to recover long-lost fitness. Norah wanted to do some volunteer work. Carl's first monthly goal was to rejoin the gym and start a weekly workout. His weekly goals included setting up a membership with the gym, booking an appointment for a fitness assessment, and attending a demonstration of how to use their new machines. Norah's first goal was to hold a bake sale in aid of a cancer charity. Week by week, Carl and Norah evaluated their progress, encouraged each other, and reviewed their techniques. A year later, he's got his six-pack back and she's working six sessions a week in a local charity shop. Both have new circles of friends and better self-esteem, and are out of their rut.

It can work for you. And if you feel discouraged sometimes, remember that PERT can also stand for Problems Eventually Resolve Themselves.

How did it go?

Q   My partner's unconvinced by your PERT idea. How can I sell it to him?

A   Try one for yourself anyway and show him the proof of the success six months from now.

Q   Is the review technique part of PERT really necessary? We made plans for our next year together and had forgotten about them. We found our plan recently while cleaning and realized we've done 90 percent of the things on our list.

A   Good for you. It sounds as if a lot of your evaluating and reviewing has been going on under the surface, even though it hasn't been formally written down. PERT is a tool, not a rule.

51

Don't know much about geography

Remember your first romance? Slipping secret love notes under the desk to your heartthrob of a schoolgirl crush? Even though school's out, you can recapture the excitement of those times.

In many relationships, most of the time one person does something and the other partner hears about it later. Attending an evening class can be a joint activity, to be done together.

LESSONS IN LOVE

So how can adult education teach you to get along better? Whatever class you pick, you'll see your partner in a new light: mingling, mixing, grappling with a new activity, or trying to assimilate new knowledge. Throwing pots together in pottery class may stop you from throwing them at each other at home. You'll be working together a lot of the time, mastering new tasks and finding out stuff you both wish you'd known before. At best, you'll become a wise and wonderful couple with a host of shared skills and memories. At the very least, it should give you some laughs on the ride home.

Here's an idea for you . . .

Not sure what evening class to join or what would suit you both? Many centers have open days or short trial courses that give you the chance to see if you both like fire-eating, information technology with business information systems, Japanese watercolor, or synchronized swimming. You'll also be able to see the teacher in action and decide whether he or she is right for you.

TRANSFERABLE SKILLS

Going back to school together can help other areas of your relationship. After attending Adventures in Advanced Accounting, Leif and Enid found they were much better at analyzing different situations and reaching creative but mutually acceptable solutions. Chuck and Martha studied counseling. Their joint work helped them distinguish between important and trivial matters in their fifteen-year relationship. Heleni and Ethel had been arguing almost every evening. At intermediate baking they had to establish an effective working partnership. Their domestic relationship has been sweeter since.

ON COURSE

Taking courses or classes together won't turn you into a motivated, enthusiastic, and hardworking couple overnight. Three weeks is more like it. But seriously, when did you two last share the sheer joy of learning for its own sake? Not to earn a certificate, not to brighten up an otherwise lackluster résumé, not to get that promotion, but learning something because the subject turns you both on? Classes provide lots of things to laugh and gossip about—and gossip is an important social lubricant in long-term relationships. Evening classes are an especially rich source: the instructor's awfulness or brilliance. Then there are the other students, a godsend for people watchers. All human life goes to evening classes: full-time moms, overachiever students, the pushy and the meek, the bright and the stupid.

Sharing some sly in-jokes and politically incorrect observations with your partner instead of just watching these diverse groups interact or fight over the one remaining computer terminal helps the two of you to bond.

Joined an evening class in the hope of extending your circle of friends and found yourself in a group you'd be glad to see the back of? Have a look at IDEA 35, *With a little help from your friends*, for other suggestions.

Try another idea . . .

HOMEWORK

The skills and knowledge acquired in adult classes need not and should not stay there. Couples who attend a Thai cooking class can feast on exotic flavors at their next romantic dinner in. Other couples who, like us, have taken a course to learn how to use a sewing machine could make over their homes with homemade soft furnishings. And if you choose courses with less tangible end products—assertiveness training or conversational Dutch—encourage each other to use your new expertise in other ways, like returning faulty items to their retailer, or going on vacation to Amsterdam.

"When you write together you end up finding out a lot about each other."
ETHAN HAWKE, actor

Defining idea . . .

"Soap and education are not as sudden as a massacre, but they are more deadly in the long run."
MARK TWAIN

Defining idea . . .

225

How did
it go?

Q **We have both enrolled in a biology course. I have to admit that the teacher is pretty awful, but my husband Keith's reaction is even worse. He is openly rude and contemptuous in the class and last week got into an argument with her. This is a side of him I have never seen before and I don't know what to do. Any suggestions?**

A *Sadly some people regress when put back in a classroom and behave like out-of-control schoolkids. When Keith has calmed down it might be worth talking to him and finding out what is going on. Given that you both accept that the teacher is lousy, you should concentrate on his overreaction and how it makes you feel. Whether biology gets the boot depends on how important it is for you both and whether you can resolve the difficulties with the teacher. We suggest you skip school and give Keith a private biology lesson at home.*

Q **We have both joined an evening class for conversational French. I'm hopeless and want to drop out, but my wife is really getting into it and wants to stay. I don't want to put a damper on her enjoyment, but it's just not working for me. What should I do?**

A *Sounds like you need to sit down and have a conversation about what is going on. Why not ask your wife to help you catch up between lessons? Make it fun: Watch a French film together, see how many food items you can name in French when you next cook dinner together, try to have a few basic conversations in French between lessons, and dance to music with French lyrics.*

226

The biggest turn-off

Looking for a quick fix for a dwindling relationship? This one's fast, free, and fantastically simple. Unplug your TV and plug in to an amazing life together.

When did you last watch something on TV that transformed your relationship for the better? Time for some home truths: It's big, it's ugly, and it rots relationships.

NOT TONIGHT, JOSEPH

Are you sick of your partner hogging the remote control? Do you continually fall asleep during soaps, reality shows, or celebrity snowboarding? Most of us recognize the damaging effect that television has on our children, but what about our love lives? We think the hold television has on society is scary. Yet the role it plays in people's lives is rarely questioned. Decades ago, broadcasts only took place in the evenings and weekend afternoons. The service closed down at midnight and what television there was, was watched on one machine in a communal area by whole families. Not anymore. The TV is taking up more and more of lovers' free time and energy. Most couples watch around four hours of television a day. Television, like a baby cuckoo, insidiously pushes everything else out of the love nest. And at what

Getting rid of the TV seems too radical? Why not have a TV-free month? Put the box, or boxes, in the attic tonight and in four-weeks time see how you did. Both keep a journal of your thoughts and feelings, and write down how you spent all that time.

Defining idea . . .

"Stare into each others eyes, or at a piece of electrical equipment? Television eats up half the time you are not working or sleeping—ten years for the average person. All those things you want to be: a lover, a parent, a scholar, a wild teenager, or a pillar of the community—when are you going to do all that? TV takes away your real life."
DAVID BURKE and JEAN LOTUS, authors of *White Dot*

Defining idea . . .

"Television? The word is half Greek, half Latin. No good can come out of it."
C. P. SCOTT, newspaper editor

cost? Is that manic machine in the corner interrupting your conversations, preventing candlelit dinners, or maybe even stopping you from trying out other ideas in this book? Whether you're channel hopping, station surfing, or really engrossed in episode 307 of that sexy sitcom, you're missing four hours a day of prime-time real life.

UNPLUG THE BOX AND PLUG INTO A WONDERFUL LIFE

When we tell people we haven't got a television, they think we're eccentric, crazy, or seriously weird. Usually they wink and ask us what we do in our evenings. We do a lot: mooch around markets, cruise on the river, see old movies on the big screen, snoop around in galleries, visit exhibitions, comedy clubs, musicals, quirky plays, and a lot of other fun stuff. We're not joined at the hip and use our bonus four hours to do lots of things on our own or with other friends. Peter likes to play squash, review books, and teach literacy to prisoners. Sabina makes jewelry, cards, glass paintings, and mosaics. We're not saying you need to do all of these things, or any of them—you need to choose the activities that would suit you. How could you recharge your relationship in a few extra hours a day? Maybe you'd like to have time to go running together, make your partner a sculpture, become part-time puppeteers, or join the local choir. Flick the off switch, get your life back, and your relationship will prosper. Whatever you do, it's better than being passive voyeurs of other peoples' lives.

Instead of vegging out in front of the TV tonight, why not wander around your neighborhood? See IDEA 3, *A walk on the wild side.*

Try another idea...

Televisions are often the focal point of our homes. Why not size up IDEA 30, *Our house*, to help you make the most of your love shack?

...and another

Now you've put down the remote control, try pressing some of your partner's buttons. See IDEA 38, *Sex.*

...and another

"Television displaces other romantic opportunities. Like brushing up against your wife's backside in the kitchen. The old-fashioned challenge of having to entertain each other."
JIM PETERSEN, author of *Playboy's History of the Sexual Revolution*

Defining idea...

229

How did it go?

Q **We think we watch far too much television and are considering getting rid of the only one we have, but we are both film buffs and would miss watching old black-and-white movies and musicals. What do you suggest?**

A *More and more movies are being released as DVDs and you can watch these on your home computer. The quality is better and you can watch them when you want rather than when the broadcasters want.*

Q **If we give up the TV we don't know what we'll talk about when we go to work or have friends over. Won't we be excluded from most conversations?**

A *That hasn't been our experience. In fact, with your exciting, busy lives, you're more likely to start conversations that workmates and friends will want to be part of. Expect to hear comments like, "You have such an interesting relationship. We never have time to do things like that." Enjoy it. We've found that the television stops a lot more conversations than it ever starts.*

Where it's at . . .

Index

52 Brilliant Ideas

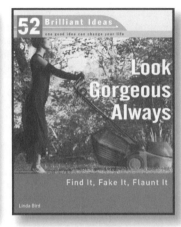

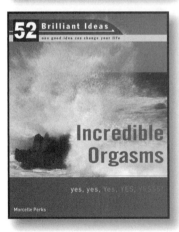

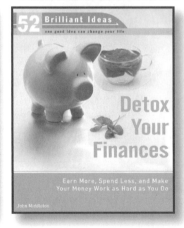

LIVE LONGER
978-0-399-53302-0 • 0-399-53302-8

INCREDIBLE ORGASMS
978-0-399-53303-7 • 0-399-53303-6

LOOK GORGEOUS ALWAYS
978-0-399-53304-4 • 0-399-53304-4

DETOX YOUR FINANCES
978-0-399-53301-3 • 0-399-53301-X

SURVIVING DIVORCE
978-0-399-53305-1 • 0-399-53305-2

**GET MARRIED
WITHOUT A HITCH**
978-0-399-53306-8 • 0-399-53306-0

PERIGEE An imprint of Penguin Group (USA)

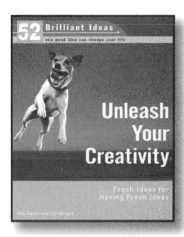